Buddhism Today

How to Be a Buddhist in the Modern World

Olivia Rivers

© **Copyright 2023 - All rights reserved.**

The content contained within this book may not be reproduced, duplicated, or transmitted without direct written permission from the author or the publisher.

Under no circumstances will any blame or legal responsibility be held against the publisher, or author, for any damages, reparation, or monetary loss due to the information contained within this book, either directly or indirectly.

Legal Notice:

This book is copyright protected. It is only for personal use. You cannot amend, distribute, sell, use, quote or paraphrase any part, or the content within this book, without the consent of the author or publisher.

Disclaimer Notice:

Please note the information contained within this document is for educational and entertainment purposes only. All effort has been executed to present accurate, up to date, reliable, complete information. No warranties of any kind are declared or implied. Readers acknowledge that the author is not engaged in the rendering of legal, financial, medical, or professional advice. The content within this book has been derived from various sources. Please consult a licensed professional before attempting any techniques outlined in this book.

By reading this document, the reader agrees that under no circumstances is the author responsible for any losses, direct or indirect, that are incurred as a result of the use of the information contained within this document, including, but not limited to, errors, omissions, or inaccuracies.

A Gift for Your Journey

Welcome to *"Buddhism Today"!*

As an expression of gratitude for being a part of this journey, I've included a special gift for you.

Scan the QR code below and follow the simple instructions to receive your complimentary copy of *"The Modern Meditator's Guidebook"*.

May this resource be a guiding light on your path to mindfulness and inner peace.

Thank you for joining me on this transformative voyage towards wisdom and compassion.

Wishing you profound revelations and boundless harmony as you embark on this enriching exploration.

'Do not dwell on the past, do not dream of the future, concentrate the mind on the present moment.'

— Gautama Buddha

Table of Contents

INTRODUCTION 1

CHAPTER 1: UNDERSTANDING BUDDHISM 3

   THE LIFE OF BUDDHA: CHILDHOOD AND ROYAL LIFE 4
      A Royal Birth 4
      The Palace: A Land of Eternal Spring 4
      Siddhartha's Inner World: The Golden Cage 5
      Fatherly Fears: King Suddhodana's Protective Measures 5
      The Contrast: Siddhartha's Spiritual Restlessness 5
   THE FOUR SIGHTS: THE TURNING POINTS THAT IGNITED A SPIRITUAL ODYSSEY 6
      The Forbidden Journey: Escaping the Palace Walls 6
      The Shock of Old Age: Crumbling Foundations 6
      The Sting of Sickness: The Fragility of Well-Being 7
      The Finality of Death: The Inescapable End 7
      The Ascetic: The Epitome of Serenity 7
      The Inner Transformation: The Four Sights as Catalysts 8
   ENLIGHTENMENT: THE DAWN OF UNSHAKABLE WISDOM AND BOUNDLESS COMPASSION 9
      The Radical Departure: Leaving behind All That Was Known 9
      The Journey into Asceticism: The Misguided Search 9
      The Turning Point: The Middle Way 9
      Under the Bodhi Tree: A Cosmic Connection 10
      The Great Awakening: Becoming the Buddha 10
   THE FOUR NOBLE TRUTHS AND EIGHTFOLD PATH: FOUNDATIONS OF BUDDHISM 11
      The First Noble Truth: Dukkha—Unsatisfactoriness 12
      The Second Noble Truth: Samudaya—The Origin of Dissatisfaction 18
      The Third Noble Truth: Nirodha—The Cessation of Dissatisfaction 22
      The Fourth Noble Truth: Magga—The Path Leading to the Cessation of Suffering 23
   AN INVITATION TO YOUR OWN AWAKENING 27

CHAPTER 2: APPLYING BUDDHISM IN THE MODERN WORLD 29

   BUDDHIST WISDOM ON MENTAL HEALTH 29

The Role of Perception in Stress Management 30
Ethical Living: A Foundation for Mental Health 31
BUDDHIST INSIGHTS INTO DECISION-MAKING 33
THE TOOLS OF BUDDHISM FOR MODERN CHALLENGES 35
Mindfulness: More than a Buzzword 35
Techniques for Incorporating Mindfulness into Daily Routines 36
The Transformative Journey through Buddhist Meditation 39
The Panorama of Buddhist Meditation 41
Incorporating Meditation into Daily Routines 45

CHAPTER 3: BUDDHISM AND ETHICS 51

THE FIVE PRECEPTS: A GUIDELINE FOR CONSCIOUS LIVING 53
First Precept: Abstain from Killing 54
Second Precept: Abstain from Stealing 56
Third Precept: Abstain from Sexual Misconduct 58
Fourth Precept: Abstain from Wrong Speech 60
Fifth Precept: Abstain from the Use of Intoxicating Substances that Cause Inattention 62
THE TEN PARAMIS 65
First Paramis: Generosity (Dāna) 68
Second Paramis: Morality (Sīla) 69
Third Paramis: Renunciation (Nekkhamma) 70
Fourth Paramis: Wisdom (Paññā) 71
Fifth Paramis: Energy (Viriya) 71
Sixth Paramis: Patience (Khanti) 72
Seventh Paramis: Truthfulness (Sacca) 73
Eighth Paramis: Determination (Adhiṭṭhāna) 74
Ninth Paramis: Loving-kindness (Mettā) 75
Tenth Paramis: Equanimity (Upekkhā) 76
RECONCILIATION OF BUDDHISM AND OTHER ETHICAL SYSTEMS 77
Hinduism 78
Judaism 79
Christianity and Catholicism 80
Islam 81
Actionable Insights for Interfaith Understanding 82

CHAPTER 4: BUDDHISM AND RELATIONSHIPS 85

BUDDHIST PRINCIPLES IN PERSONAL RELATIONSHIPS 85
FRIENDSHIP THROUGH A BUDDHIST LENS 87
Embracing the "No-Self" in Conflict Resolution with Friends 88
Mindful Communication and Reflective Dialogue 89

Celebrating Others' Joy through Interdependence 89
Understanding Codependency and Karma in Friendships 90
NURTURING FAMILIAL BONDS THROUGH BUDDHISM 91
Transforming Difficult Marriage: The Tale of Chieko Yamashita ... 92
ROMANTIC RELATIONSHIPS IN BUDDHISM 94
Finding and Nurturing Relationships 94
Navigating Relationship Challenges 96

CHAPTER 5: BUDDHISM AND TECHNOLOGY 99

A JOURNEY THROUGH TIME: BUDDHISM AND TECHNOLOGICAL EVOLUTION 100
Ancient Wisdom Meets Scientific Endeavors 100
Woodblock Printing: A Revolution Fostered by Buddhism 101
A Guiding Light in Today's Tech-Driven World 102
THE DANGERS OF OVERCONSUMPTION 102
THE PARADOX OF SEEKING MINDFULNESS IN A TECH-DRIVEN WORLD 104
BALANCING TECHNOLOGY USE WITH BUDDHIST PRINCIPLES 105
The Middle Path Approach to Technology 106
Mindful Consumption of Content 107
Setting Boundaries: Digital Detoxes and Mindful Tech Breaks 107
Harnessing Technology for Spiritual Growth 108

CHAPTER 6: BUDDHISM AND ENVIRONMENTALISM 111

A BRIEF HISTORY OF ENVIRONMENTAL CONSCIOUSNESS IN BUDDHIST TEXTS 112
THE CORE OF BUDDHIST ENVIRONMENTALISM 113
THE BUDDHIST APPROACH TO MODERN ENVIRONMENTAL CHALLENGES 114
PRACTICAL ACTIONS ROOTED IN BUDDHIST PRINCIPLES 116
Building a Sustainable Lifestyle 116
Guided Mindfulness and Meditation Exercises to Reconnect with Nature 118

CHAPTER 7: PRACTICING BUDDHISM TODAY 121

BUILDING AND FINDING BUDDHIST COMMUNITIES 122
The Joy and Benefits of a Shared Spiritual Journey 123
Creating a Space for Collective Growth and Learning 124
THE SOLITARY PRACTITIONER 126
Crafting a Personal Spiritual Routine 126
Online Platforms and Resources 127
INTERFAITH DIALOGUE AND BALANCING BELIEFS 127
Begin with Common Ground 129
Listen Respectfully 129
Educate and Be Willing to Be Educated 129

Practice Mindful Communication *130*
Participate in Collaborative Projects *130*
Engage in Personal Reflection *130*
Exhibit Patience and Perseverance *131*

CHAPTER 8: ENLIGHTENMENT AND BUDDHIST GOAL 133

The Essence of Enlightenment 134
Historical Significance: The Buddha's Journey 135
A Universal Potential 135
The Modern Search for Enlightenment 136
Preparing the Mind and Heart 138
Letting Go: The Art of "No-Self" and Detachment *139*
Enlightenment in Daily Life 140

CONCLUSION 143

EMBRACE YOUR JOURNEY 147

REFERENCES 149

Introduction

Have you ever paused in the midst of a busy day to wonder if there's a deeper, more serene layer to life waiting to be discovered? Have you come across the word "Buddhism" and felt a flicker of curiosity about what this tradition could offer in today's hyper-connected, swiftly changing world?

At first glance, Buddhism, a tradition founded around the 5th century BCE, might seem a world away from the realities of our digital age. Yet, as we grapple with existential challenges such as climate change and mental health crises, the teachings of Siddhartha Gautama (known as the Buddha) have never been more pertinent.

Buddhism has navigated vast temporal, cultural, and geographical landscapes, stretching from the serene origin valleys of India to bustling cities worldwide. Just as the 71-meter tall monumental Buddha statue in Sichuan, China (carved in the 8th century) has withstood the test of time, the principles of Buddhism remain unshaken amidst the winds of change. Its foundational teachings offer profound insights into human suffering and the path to its cessation. It's no wonder that even in today's society—characterized by technological advancements and constant connectivity—the essence of these teachings remains a beacon for many seeking serenity and wisdom.

In our contemporary context, where time is fragmented by a thousand online distractions, the very act of mindfulness (a core Buddhist practice) emerges as a revolutionary act. But how do we practice it authentically? How do we embody compassion in an era of viral outrage? How do the Buddhist principles of nonattachment, impermanence, and interdependence assist us in navigating modern challenges like rampant consumerism, climate change, and social inequality? Can we, amidst our data-driven routines, still embark on a quest for enlightenment?

Buddhism Today: How to Be a Buddhist in the Modern World takes you on an enlightening journey through these very questions. Beginning with the captivating life story of Buddha, we'll delve deep into the core principles of Buddhism, making them relatable and actionable for today's readers. We'll explore the fusion of ancient wisdom with modern lifestyles, from the ways Buddhism can enhance our mental health to its intersection with technology, relationships, and environmentalism. Each chapter offers an opportunity for reflection and self-discovery; enriched with real-life examples, exercises, and stories that bring the teachings to life.

Whether you walk the path of a practicing Buddhist, seek spiritual enlightenment, or simply yearn for tranquility in a turbulent world, this book extends a heartfelt invitation. It's not merely a journey of learning; it's an inspiring voyage of living. It's about realizing how the profound serenity embodied by the still, stone figure of Buddha can become a vibrant reality even in the midst of our fast-paced, digitalized world.

So, as you turn the pages, I invite you to approach with an open heart and a curious mind. Welcome to *Buddhism Today*, where the journey of enlightenment and wisdom awaits.

Chapter 1:

Understanding Buddhism

In our ever-evolving world, with its myriad beliefs and practices, the teachings of Buddhism remain timeless; offering solace, clarity, and guidance. To truly grasp the profundity of Buddhism, one must journey to its origins and explore the life of its founder: Siddhartha Gautama, who later became the Buddha. The early episodes from Siddhartha's life, his encounters with the realities of existence, and his pursuit of enlightenment offer invaluable lessons for all.

In this chapter, sourced extensively from the Buddho.org (n.d.) website—a foundation inspired by the spirit of Theravāda Buddhism—we dive deep into the heart of these teachings. Theravāda, which translates as the "School of the Elders," is one of the oldest extant schools of Buddhism. It has meticulously preserved Gautama Buddha's teachings in the Pāli Canon.

We embark on our peregrination from the tranquil backdrop of Siddhartha's royal birthplace, venturing into the opulent corridors of his palace. It appeared to be a perfect world, yet it felt like a gilded cage to the young prince. As we peel back the layers, we encounter the transformative episodes known as the "Four Sights," acting as catalysts, propelling Siddhartha toward his ultimate enlightenment under the Bodhi tree. This awakening gave birth to the foundational pillars of Buddhism: The Four Noble Truths and the Noble Eightfold Path.

Join us on this enlightening journey where ancient tales interweave with universal truths; offering insights into our own quests for meaning, peace, and spiritual growth. As you read, may you find resonance with the lessons of the past, and inspiration for the present.

The Life of Buddha: Childhood and Royal Life

A Royal Birth

Siddhartha Gautama was not just born into luxury; his birth itself was considered miraculous. According to legend, his mother, Queen Maya, dreamt of a white elephant descending from heaven and entering her womb. When Siddhartha was born, it is said that he took seven steps and declared that this would be his last birth. Astrologers predicted he would either become a great king or a spiritual leader. This intriguing blend of the mystical and the opulent set the stage for Siddhartha's complex relationship with material wealth and spiritual fulfillment.

The Palace: A Land of Eternal Spring

Imagine living in a place designed to be an eternal spring, where the chill of suffering never touches you. That's what the palace in Kapilavastu was like. Orchards bloomed year-round, musicians played melodious tunes, and dancers entertained the royals. Siddhartha had the best tutors and enjoyed games and scholarly debates with other noble children. It was a childhood that most could only dream of—yet, as physically gratifying as it was, it was also emotionally and spiritually stifling.

Siddhartha's Inner World: The Golden Cage

Siddhartha had everything a young prince could desire: Clothes woven from the finest fabrics, sumptuous meals, and even a beautiful wife named Yasodhara. Yet, a gnawing sense of dissatisfaction persisted. Have you ever felt restless despite having every comfort? Siddhartha's life is an extreme example of how external circumstances can't quench an internal thirst. In his case, the thirst wasn't for water or wine but for something deeper—meaning, purpose, and truth.

Fatherly Fears: King Suddhodana's Protective Measures

The king, who wanted to keep his son safe and on the path to becoming his successor, heard prophecies about Siddhartha's possible departure from royal life. Imagine being so afraid of losing something that you inadvertently smother it. King Suddhodana erected emotional and physical walls around Siddhartha. He kept the harsh realities of life—like aging, sickness, and death—away from the young prince. However, these well-intentioned safeguards transformed into veils of ignorance that Siddhartha sought to uncover, which served as the driving force behind his quest to understand the world.

The Contrast: Siddhartha's Spiritual Restlessness

So, here's Siddhartha, enveloped in all this luxury, yet as restless as a caged bird. It's easy to think that if we just have "one more thing," our lives would be complete. But Siddhartha had all the "things" and yet felt incomplete. His soul was like a parched land awaiting the rain of enlightenment. As I mentioned before, it's this irony—the tension between what Siddhartha had and what he felt he needed—that would become the catalyst for his eventual journey toward enlightenment.

The Four Sights: The Turning Points That Ignited a Spiritual Odyssey

The Forbidden Journey: Escaping the Palace Walls

Picture this: Siddhartha, in a chariot, slipping away from the palace under the veil of secrecy, urged by an inner voice whispering, *"There's more out there. Go, see for yourself."* His charioteer, moved by the prince's sincere quest, agreed to this risky expedition beyond the palace walls. It was as though the universe itself conspired to grant Siddhartha the freedom he so desperately longed for, offering him a glimpse of the real world to initiate his profound transformation.

The Shock of Old Age: Crumbling Foundations

The first jolt came when Siddhartha saw an old man, frail and bent, hobbling along the road. Remember, Siddhartha had never seen old age before. To him, this was a revelation, an unraveling of his belief that life was an eternal spring. Imagine the ground beneath you crumbling as you realize that the future holds not just promises but also the inevitable decay of body and mind. This revelation shook him to his core, sowing seeds of contemplation on the impermanence of life.

The Sting of Sickness: The Fragility of Well-Being

The second sight was that of a person tormented by illness, writhing in pain. Siddhartha had lived in such a sheltered existence that sickness was a foreign concept. As he witnessed the anguish of illness, he realized that his own body, the vessel he had taken for granted, was not invulnerable but rather quite limited and fragile. The encounter laid bare the vulnerability of human existence, underscoring that suffering was not a possibility but a certainty in life.

The Finality of Death: The Inescapable End

The third sight was perhaps the most unsettling of all—a corpse, surrounded by grieving family members. Siddhartha was struck by the permanence of death, the ultimate cessation of all experiences. For the first time, he faced the harsh reality that life's complexities, joys, and even sufferings have an expiration date. For Siddhartha, this unsettling epiphany mirrored embarking on a once-blissful journey that ultimately led to a precipitous plunge into the unknown, where understanding and purpose remained elusive.

The Ascetic: The Epitome of Serenity

The final sight was a stark contrast to the preceding ones—an ascetic, radiant with inner peace, devoid of any material possessions. Now, you might be wondering, what exactly is an ascetic? Think of an ascetic as someone who gives up life's comforts and luxuries on purpose. They live simply, often choosing not to indulge in things like tasty food, fancy clothes, or even a cozy home. They do this to focus inward, to find a sense of peace and understanding that doesn't rely on external factors.

This encounter provided Siddhartha with a glimmer of hope. The ascetic seemed to have transcended the suffering that seemed so inescapable. Could there be a way out after all? Could living simply, like this ascetic, offer a path to serenity? This figure posed an answer to the existential questions that had been tormenting him.

By meeting this ascetic, Siddhartha began to contemplate the possibility that there might be an alternate path of existence—a path that cuts through the noise and confusion of life to find something deeper and more meaningful. It's like when we declutter our homes to create space for what truly matters; this ascetic had decluttered his life. This notion sparked a question in Siddhartha's mind: Could this be the path to comprehension and serenity?

The Inner Transformation: The Four Sights as Catalysts

The Four Sights weren't just external encounters; they were reflections of Siddhartha's inner turmoil. They were his reality checks, confrontations that forced him to reevaluate what he knew—or thought he knew—about life. It's like reading a profound book or having an enlightening conversation that changes the way you see the world. For Siddhartha, these experiences were turning points that set him on a path toward deeper understanding and, eventually, enlightenment.

Enlightenment: The Dawn of Unshakable Wisdom and Boundless Compassion

The Radical Departure: Leaving behind All That Was Known

Imagine waking up one morning and realizing that everything you've built your life around—family, social status, wealth—won't ultimately bring you true happiness. Siddhartha felt a moral imperative to seek the antidote to life's existential dilemmas. To do this, he did what most of us would consider unthinkable: He left behind his family, his home, and his future as a ruler. It's like abandoning a scripted life to pen a new, uncertain narrative, guided by an inner compass of truth-seeking.

The Journey into Asceticism: The Misguided Search

Eager to find answers, Siddhartha immersed himself in rigorous ascetic practices. He thought that by denying the body, he could elevate the mind. Imagine punishing your body, thinking that this self-inflicted suffering would lead to enlightenment. It was a sincere but misplaced effort. After years of austere living, Siddhartha was skeletal and weakened, but no closer to the truth he sought.

The Turning Point: The Middle Way

Realizing that neither the luxurious life of the palace nor the self-denial of asceticism had brought him peace, Siddhartha thought of a different path—the Middle Way. This approach highlights the importance of finding a balanced middle ground between indulgence and deprivation. It emphasizes that a fulfilling life can be achieved by maintaining equilibrium, allowing you to enjoy life's pleasures in moderation while exercising self-discipline without feeling restricted.

Under the Bodhi Tree: A Cosmic Connection

Then came the fateful night under the Bodhi tree, where Siddhartha engaged in deep meditation. He sat as if he were anchoring himself to the earth, seeking a profound connection with the cosmos—a convergence of his mind with the universe itself. In this profound state of meditation, layers of ignorance began to slowly peel away. It was as though a veil that had clouded his understanding for so long was gradually lifting. With each layer shed, Siddhartha's mind became clearer and more illuminated, much like the first rays of dawn breaking through the darkness of the night.

The Great Awakening: Becoming the Buddha

It was here, nested in the lap of nature, that Siddhartha became the Buddha, the "Awakened One." He grasped the Four Noble Truths—the essence of existence encapsulated in the realities of suffering, its cause, its cessation, and the path to achieving that cessation. He also laid down the Eightfold Path, a practical guide for ethical and mental development. This wasn't merely a flicker of insight; it marked a profound transformation—a metamorphosis from a seeker into an awakened being, fully attuned to the intrinsic essence of life and reality.

The Four Noble Truths and Eightfold Path: Foundations of Buddhism

At the core of what we now call Buddhism—or, as it was referred to in ancient times, the **Dhamma-Vinaya**—are teachings that provide pragmatic guidance for those yearning for wisdom, ethical conduct, and mental discipline. Siddhartha Gautama, after becoming the Buddha or "The Awakened One," felt an immense responsibility to share the liberating truths he had discovered.

The teachings that poured forth from him weren't esoteric philosophical concepts, but a profound roadmap accessible to anyone willing to walk the path of enlightenment. This universal guide is summarized in the Four Noble Truths—a set of teachings that serve as a compass for navigating life's turbulence.

Think of the Four Noble Truths as foundational pillars holding up the structure of Buddhist philosophy. They aren't just theoretical principles, but applicable life lessons. Like the force of gravity, these truths are constant, governing every life regardless of background, culture, or belief system. They offer guidelines that help us understand and navigate the complexities of human existence, characterized by **dukkha**—a term that embodies the pervasive unsatisfactoriness, suffering, or stress we all encounter.

At the heart of the Dhamma-Vinaya, which encompasses the Buddha's teachings and ethical guidelines, lies the concept of morality, known as **Vinaya**. Just as **Dhamma (or Dharma)** encapsulates the ultimate truth and the teachings of the Buddha, Vinaya represents the moral framework essential for walking the path to liberation. This underscores the importance of ethical conduct as not just an optional practice but a vital part of achieving liberation from suffering.

Over the centuries, diverse Buddhist schools have emerged due to historical and cultural influences, each presenting varying ethical, philosophical, and practical dimensions. Yet, they all share a common core—The Four Noble Truths: The truth of suffering, the truth of the origin of suffering, the truth of the cessation of suffering, and the path that leads to the cessation of suffering.

Whether you identify as a Buddhist or not, these truths touch upon the core realities of human experience. They offer invaluable insights into the human condition, providing practical tools to deal with life's challenges, find inner peace, and ultimately, achieve liberation from the cycle of craving and dissatisfaction.

The First Noble Truth: Dukkha—Unsatisfactoriness

Let's delve deeper into the Noble Truths and the first one is the truth of dukkha, often translated as suffering or unsatisfactoriness. The Buddha, in his first teaching, stated, "Birth is suffering, aging is suffering, illness is suffering, death is suffering; union with what is displeasing is suffering; separation from what is pleasing is suffering; not to get what one wants is suffering; in brief, the five aggregates subject to clinging are suffering."

When the Buddha delved into the concept of "dukkha," he was imparting a profound insight into the nature of existence. He likened life to a rollercoaster, a metaphor that vividly captures its inherent fluctuations, replete with both exhilarating highs and challenging lows. These experiences aren't limited to physical discomforts like stubbing a toe or enduring a headache; they also encompass the emotional turbulence that we all encounter.

Feelings of stress, anxiety, or disappointment can wash over us like a sudden downpour. In essence, life can offer joy, but it can also throw curveballs that make you feel like you're stuck in a rain cloud.

The five aggregates (khandhas) Buddha mentions include:

1. **Matter (rūpa)**: This represents the physical aspect of existence, the material body, and the external physical world around us. It's the tangible, touchable aspect of our world.

2. **Feeling (vedanā)**: These are the raw sensations experienced through contact of the six faculties (eyes, ears, nose, tongue, body, and mind) with their respective external phenomena. This can include feelings of pleasure, pain, or neither pleasure nor pain.

3. **Perception (saññā)**: Also referred to as cognition, perception is the mental ability to recognize and label physical and mental phenomena, distinguishing and identifying different objects. For instance, when you see a red apple, your mind says, "That's an apple, and it's red." It helps you make sense of the world.

4. **Mental formations (saṅkhāras)**: This encompasses a wide array of mental activities, including volition, intention, attention, and desires. It includes all kinds of mental habits, thoughts, ideas, opinions, prejudices, compulsions, and decisions triggered by an object. It includes everything from your grand ambitions to why you prefer chocolate over vanilla.

5. **Consciousness (viññāṇa)**: This is a very broad term that encompasses the basic awareness of a sensory input plus the perception of its associated mental objects. It's referred to as the mind's ability to know or "be aware,"

encompassing a range of cognitive processes including the collection of sensory information, processing it, and generating responses. It's how you know you're experiencing life right now.

These elements were considered to encompass everything in the world during the time of the Buddha. However, the Buddha suggested that holding on too tightly to any of these components can lead to suffering. This underlines the far-reaching implications of his words.

In the same way, Buddha's idea of dukkha isn't just about the big, obvious kinds of suffering like grief or pain. It's also about the subtle, ongoing discomfort that happens when life isn't going quite your way—similar to a wheel that's misaligned and causes a bumpy ride. So, you'll find three types of this dukkha:

1. **Directly experienced suffering (dukkha-dukkhata)**: This is straightforward pain or discomfort, including both mental and physical pain, such as the physical discomfort of bumping your toe or the mental pain of grief caused by the loss of a loved one.

2. **Suffering as a result of change (viparinama-dukkha)**: Refers to the suffering of the pleasurable experience itself because everything that arises will eventually pass away, leading to potential suffering. So, it happens when something good turns bad. Imagine enjoying your favorite meal and then discovering an unexpected and unpleasant taste or ingredient in the dish. This shift from delight to discomfort illustrates how change can bring about suffering, especially when something pleasurable unexpectedly transforms into an unpleasant experience.

3. **Suffering inherent in all conditioned states (saṅkhāra-dukkha)**: This is the most subtle type—it's

like a low-level buzz of dissatisfaction that you can't quite put your finger on, present even when everything seems fine. The continuous underlying dissatisfaction within existence at the deepest level. As long as there are conditions, existence continues, leading to endless wandering in samsāra (the cycle of rebirth).

Samsāra and the Cycle of Existence

The concept of samsāra, the "endless wandering," is crucial to understanding dukkha. Samsāra represents the continuous cycle of life and death, constantly subject to suffering due to desire. The Buddha emphasized that there is no beginning to this cycle, and even death does not offer a permanent solution.

He introduced three pivotal ideas to navigate through samsāra, which are also known as the three marks (or characteristics) of existence: The truths of impermanence (anicca), unsatisfactoriness (dukkha), and the lack of selflessness (anattā). Realizing that everything around us constantly changes, life inherently contains challenges, and our notion of "self" is much more fluid than we believe, can provide us the tools to transcend these cyclical patterns.

We already touched upon the concept of dukkha, but let's discuss each of these characteristics. Understanding them can truly shift the way we engage with our world, offering a fresh perspective on our experiences. This also connects with the knowledge of the transient and interdependent nature of the five aggregates, which as we learned, are the building blocks of what we usually perceive as the "self."

1. **Impermanence (anicca)**: This concept is often summed up as "all that has arisen will pass away." Just like the tree and its seasons, everything in life is constantly changing. This recognition of the rise and fall

15

of things from moment to moment, with such speed that it seems like a continuous stream, is crucial for developing insight and wisdom.

2. **Unsatisfaction or suffering (dukkha)**: As we've learned, dukkha is one of the fundamental realities of existence. But to simply label it as "suffering" may not capture its entirety. Dukkha encompasses everything from the most acute pain to the most subtle feelings of discontent. It's the anxiety about an uncertain future, the pang of nostalgia for a past that's gone, the sting of unmet expectations, and the yearning for things to be different than they are. While physical pain is an evident form of dukkha, the more subtle forms often elude our notice. It's the itch of boredom when we have a quiet moment, the restlessness of wanting more even when we have enough, and the unease that lingers even during seemingly happy moments, hinting that they might not last.

3. **Selflessness or not-self (anattā)**: Recognizing impermanence naturally leads to understanding the other principle of selflessness (anattā). This principle teaches us that the sense of self is an illusion. It's the idea that the individual self does not exist in the way we think it does. Think of a car. We consider a car as one entity, but when deconstructed, it's just a collection of parts—wheels, engine, frame, etc. When the parts come together, we regard it as a "car," but none of the elements by themselves are a "car." The same applies to an individual. We are not one entity, but a collection of parts—body, feelings, perceptions, mental formations, and consciousness.

But why do we experience dukkha? The Buddha taught that its roots lie in our cravings and aversions. When we cling to certain feelings, people, or material things, expecting them to provide

16

lasting happiness, we set ourselves up for disappointment. Everything is impermanent (anicca), so any attachment will eventually lead to suffering when change occurs.

Moreover, our misunderstanding of the concept of self (anattā) feeds into our experience of dukkha. We believe in the illusion of a constant "I" and define ourselves based on the five aggregates. This misperception leads to a continuous cycle of craving, attachment, and, inevitably, suffering.

Increasing awareness of dukkha might seem counterintuitive, as it may initially appear to increase suffering. However, those who become increasingly aware of the reality of dukkha can derive tremendous energy and motivation to make the necessary effort to end it, as ending suffering is possible!

Consider you're in a boat with a small leak. Ignoring the leak because it's small would eventually sink the boat. Dukkha is like that leak. Recognizing it empowers you to patch it up so you can navigate the turbulent waters of life with more resilience and ease.

The First Noble Truth isn't about getting overwhelmed by life's challenges; instead, it's about attaining the wisdom to perceive the world with clear and unclouded eyes, free from misconceptions. Only by acknowledging that the boat leaks can you begin the work of fixing it, setting the stage for a journey toward calm waters and sunny skies.

The Second Noble Truth: Samudaya—The Origin of Dissatisfaction

The Second Noble Truth revolves around understanding the origins of dukkha. At the core of this suffering is desire or craving (tanha), which describes the relentless pursuit of something outside ourselves, whether it's material possessions, approval from others, or a sense of identity. It's like trying to fill a bottomless pit—no matter how much you put in, it will never seem full.

To understand it better, think of those moments when you've earnestly yearned for something or wished for change to appear in one form or another. It could be a tangible item, a life situation, or even a feeling. This very desire—or, more specifically, the craving we harbor—is what Buddhism identifies as the core reason for our dissatisfaction.

According to the Buddha, the root of our suffering, or dissatisfaction, is this craving that we continually experience. But this sensation isn't limited to just desiring something; it also encompasses the aversion to certain experiences. It's like having an itch. Whether we want to get rid of an itch (not wanting) or yearn for the pleasure of scratching the itch (wanting), both sentiments spring from the same source: desire.

Our senses play a significant role in this. We have six senses: Sight, hearing, smell, taste, touch, and even our thoughts. Each sense connects with objects that can be delightful or unpleasant, leading us to either desire them or push them away.

For instance, we might crave the sweet taste of chocolate or want to avoid the pungent smell of rotten food. Even our thoughts, dreams, opinions, and concepts can create desires. Ever craved a dream job? Or wished for a moment from the past to return?

That's your mind, counted as one of the senses in Buddhism, at work.

The Buddha's teaching reveals three main forms of desire:

1. **Sensory Desire (kāma-taṇhā)**: This is the most basic form and revolves around our senses. It's not only about erotic or sensual desires but encompasses all forms of wanting or not wanting that spring from our senses' interaction with the world.

2. **Desire for Eternal Existence (bhava-taṇhā)**: This goes beyond the surface longing, like wishing for an afterlife. It's the deep-rooted yearning for "being." It might sound complex, but at its heart, it's the hope or belief in some eternal, unchanging self.

3. **Desire for Non-Existence (vibhava-taṇhā)**: The wish for self-destruction or the end of being. It might stem from a belief that after death, there's just emptiness, but it's crucial to differentiate this from the genuine Buddhist aspiration to end the cycle of birth and rebirth (samsāra). Truly, the key to ending suffering is understanding the true essence of everything, which leads to the elimination of desire. As long as any form of desire remains, life keeps moving forward, from one moment to the next and from one lifetime to another.

Karma

At the very core of the Buddhist doctrine lies a fundamental concept: karma. To truly grasp the profound interconnectedness that the teachings emphasize, let's delve into what karma really means.

Karma, a term many might've heard in passing or popular culture, is deeper than just the consequences of our actions. Derived from the Pali word "kamma," it's centered around intention. Think of karma as the energy we set into motion with every intention we hold and act upon. Every thought, word, and deed is infused with the power of intention, and this is the very seed of karma. It's like setting a ball in motion—the initial push (the intention) determines its trajectory (the outcome). This is integral to the intricate web of causality depicted in the doctrine of **dependent origination**.

When we examine the cause of dissatisfaction in our lives, we identify desire as a significant culprit. This desire stems from ignorance—a lack of true understanding. Which begs the question: How can mere desire lead to suffering and the cycle of rebirth? Here's where dependent origination comes into play. It—along with the Four Noble Truths—lays the foundation for the Dhamma, the teachings of the Buddha.

Our everyday experiences can be likened to watching a film. To the naked eye, a movie seems fluid, with the story, visuals, and music creating an immersive experience. But if you were to dissect it, you'd realize it's a series of images and sounds pieced together at high speed. Similarly, our perceptions—seeing, hearing, tasting, touching—are not continuous but a rapid succession of individual moments. And it's in understanding these moments where we find karma at work.

Each of these moments has an intention behind it, an energy. And this energy (also known as karma) plays a role in the larger web of causality, or dependent origination. Each fragment of our perception is connected to another, each moment influences the next. Imagine dominoes lined up. The push to one (intention or karma) sets off a chain reaction.

In his teachings on dependent origination, the Buddha painted a clear picture of this causal chain: Ignorance leads to volitional formations (essentially, our intentions or karma), which in turn leads to consciousness, then name-and-form, following through to the six sense bases (contact, feeling, craving, clinging, and so on), culminating in birth, aging, and death. This cycle is what keeps us tethered to the wheel of existence, perpetually moving from one life to the next.

But here's the silver lining: Just as this chain is set into motion with ignorance and desire, its cessation is possible with understanding and the fading away of ignorance. This is the hope the Buddha's message offers.

To fully grasp karma's role, we must address some misconceptions. Karma isn't destiny or punishment meted out by some higher power. Instead, it's the energy of our intentions playing out in various ways, influenced by various conditions. This isn't about "bad" or "good" karma—it's about understanding that every intention sets forth an energy that has repercussions.

It's neither a rigid one-to-one system nor is it arbitrary. Like seeds in a garden, the fruits they bear depend on various conditions like soil, water, and sunlight. Similarly, the outcomes of our karmic actions are influenced by past actions, current intentions, and other myriad factors.

Karma and rebirth are intertwined concepts in Buddhism. But rebirth doesn't imply the migration of a soul. Rather, it's the continuation of the energy—the karmic force—from one life to another. Picture a candle lighting another. The flame is transferred, not the wax or the wick. Similarly, the karmic energy moves forward and attaches itself to new existences.

Understanding karma is paramount in our journey through Buddhist teachings. As we become more mindful of our intentions and actions, we slowly navigate the vast web of dependent origination, inching closer to liberation. And in this wisdom lies the true essence of the Buddha's teachings.

In essence, the Second Noble Truth invites us to understand our desires, recognize their origins, and realize that by addressing the root—ignorance and craving—we can pave the path toward alleviating dissatisfaction. The teaching isn't about suppressing our desires but understanding them. By acknowledging the very nature of our desires and their origins, we can better navigate the challenges they present, leading to a more harmonious and peaceful life.

The Third Noble Truth: Nirodha—The Cessation of Dissatisfaction

The Third Noble Truth presents a refreshing perspective on life's challenges. While we often feel entangled in cycles of longing and discontent, this truth enlightens us to the idea that we don't have to remain trapped. It's akin to understanding that, even though we might frequently find ourselves caught in rainstorms of discontent, there exists a shelter we can reach.

It's essential to grasp that this isn't just a theoretical concept or an abstract promise. The Third Noble Truth is a tangible affirmation, based on the wisdom of ages, that there's a viable route to peace and contentment. It's a reminder that while the burdens of life are real and often challenging, they are not eternal chains binding us.

This truth doesn't merely hint at the possibility of cessation of suffering but boldly announces it. It encourages us to shift our focus from the relentless cycle of wanting and disappointment to the genuine potential for liberation.

Moreover, this understanding isn't about suppressing or ignoring our desires. Instead, it's about recognizing the nature of our cravings and the resulting dissatisfaction. By truly understanding the cause of our unease, we become better equipped to address it.

In essence, the Third Noble Truth doesn't only diagnose the problem but also introduces the optimism that healing and transformation are within reach. It sets the stage for the practical steps to achieve this transformation, which is beautifully laid out in the Fourth Noble Truth.

The Fourth Noble Truth: Magga—The Path Leading to the Cessation of Suffering

The Fourth Noble Truth is the prescription, the remedy to the human condition of dukkha. It's the path that guides us out of the recurring cycle of birth, suffering, and death. This path is known as the **Noble Eightfold Path**. It's like a map, detailing the directions we should take, the values we should embody, and the perspectives we should adopt to lead a life free from the chains of craving and ignorance.

The Noble Eightfold Path

The Buddha outlined the Eightfold Path as follows:

1. **Right View (sammā diṭṭhi)**: The journey begins with Right View—seeing the world as it is, not as you wish it to be. This means accepting the reality of dukkha, the causes of suffering, and the potential for liberation through the Four Noble Truths. It's like putting on a pair of glasses that help you see life more clearly, enabling you to make better decisions.

2. **Right Intention (sammā saṅkappa)**: Right Intention is the resolve to act out of kindness, compassion, and

understanding rather than from greed, hatred, or delusion. This means setting your internal compass to point toward actions that generate peace and goodwill.

3. **Right Speech (sammā vācā)**: This principle emphasizes speaking truthfully, kindly, and constructively. Picture how different your relationships would be if your words were always chosen to support, uplift, and enlighten.

4. **Right Action (sammā kammanta)**: Right Action involves behaving in ways that are ethical, respectful, and compassionate. It's having a code of conduct that includes not harming others, stealing, or engaging in deceitful behavior.

5. **Right Livelihood (sammā ājīva)**: In Right Livelihood, we are encouraged to earn a living ethically and beneficially for all. Think of it as choosing a career path that not only financially supports you but also aligns with your values and positively contributes to society.

6. **Right Effort (sammā vāyāma)**: Right Effort is the endeavor to cultivate positive habits and abandon unwholesome ones. It's the energy we invest in our personal growth and spiritual development, much like how an athlete trains to improve performance.

7. **Right Mindfulness (sammā sati)**: Mindfulness is a state of full awareness of the present moment, without judgment. It's being an impartial observer of your thoughts, feelings, and actions, helping you gain insights into your habits and tendencies.

8. **Right Concentration (sammā samādhi)**: Right Concentration refers to the practice of focused meditation, where you train your mind to stay centered on a single point of attention. This is the pinnacle of

24

mental discipline, akin to a musician who practices to master their instrument.

When distilled, these eight factors are grouped under three primary practices: **Morality** (which includes Right Speech, Right Action, and Right Livelihood), **Concentration** (comprising Right Effort, Right Mindfulness, and Right Concentration), and **Wisdom** (encompassing Right View and Right Intention).

Nibbāna: The Ultimate Goal

Recognizing that we are ensnared in the ceaseless cycle of Samsāra—the continuous loop of birth, death, and rebirth—can awaken a potent energy within us, driving a profound desire for liberation. This yearning propels us toward the unparalleled tranquility of Nibbāna (or Nirvana in Sanskrit), the ultimate pinnacle of spiritual realization in Buddhism.

Describing Nibbāna is often like trying to convey the taste of a mango to someone who has never sampled it. The Buddha himself often refrained from defining it in its entirety, suggesting that it's something one must experience firsthand to truly grasp.

At its core, Nibbāna translates as "to go out" like a fire and "to cool" (Fronsdal, 2006). It embodies the notion of extinguishing the "fires" of desire, hatred, and ignorance. By dispelling these emotional and psychological states, our First Noble Truth of dukkha comes to an end, marking a person's "awakening" or the achievement of "enlightenment."

Contrary to some beliefs, Nibbāna isn't a place, like heaven or paradise. It's a transcendent state of existence that often defies ordinary human understanding, precisely because it's beyond our worldly experiences and concepts. Despite its elusive nature,

Nibbāna can be described in positive terms, embodying ultimate peace, supreme happiness, and the pinnacle of reality.

One pivotal aspect of Nibbāna is its nature of selflessness or "not-self" (anattā). Rather than the fusion of self with a greater reality, it is the profound realization that there isn't a persistent self to start with. Everyday perceptions are often rooted in an "I" standpoint, leading us to continuously differentiate ourselves from others, setting the stage for discord.

By understanding this "I" standpoint and the illusory nature of the self, we circle back to the First Noble Truth, recognizing that the inherent dukkha in our lives is intrinsically linked to our misperceptions of existence. As we delve deeper into the teachings, we see the interconnectedness of these concepts, revealing a roadmap to inner peace and liberation.

However, through understanding the three core characteristics of existence (impermanence/anicca, unsatisfactoriness/dukkha, and selflessness/anattā), we uncover a gateway to transcend this cycle. By ardently treading the Noble Eightfold Path—the comprehensive roadmap encompassing understanding, intention, speech, action, livelihood, effort, mindfulness, and concentration—practitioners endeavor to grasp Nibbāna, which stands as the apex goal in numerous Buddhist traditions.

On this spiritual path, you'll progress through various stages of insight and growth. It begins with a simple introduction to enlightenment, and over time, you'll advance to the most enlightened state known as **Arahant**. With every stage, your comprehension deepens, guiding you nearer to a life free from suffering and filled with peace.

An Invitation to Your Own Awakening

As we go about our lives, we may not experience cosmic transformations under a Bodhi tree, but we do have our moments of quiet reflection, times when we question the status quo and seek deeper understanding. The story of the Buddha's enlightenment invites us to embark on our own spiritual journeys, whatever they may be.

It reassures us that enlightenment isn't reserved for a chosen few—it's a path open to anyone brave enough to question, seek, and practice. So, in the midst of your own challenges, uncertainties, and quests for meaning, remember the Buddha's journey from ignorance to enlightenment. It serves as both inspiration and a roadmap for all of us in search of a life filled with greater wisdom and compassion.

As we transition from the pages of ancient wisdom to the bustling lanes of our modern world, one might wonder: *How do these ancient teachings fit into our 21st-century lives? Is it possible to carry the torch of Buddha's wisdom amid our tech-driven routines, our digital distractions, and the relentless pace of change?* The answer is a resounding yes.

In the chapters ahead, we'll demystify the art of integrating Buddhist principles into our daily existence. From mindfulness exercises for improved productivity to compassionate strategies for navigating complex relationships, we'll discover that the core tenets of Buddhism are not just historical anecdotes, but timeless tools for personal and societal transformation.

Imagine cultivating inner peace while surrounded by city skyscrapers or finding moments of Zen amid the ping of smartphone notifications. It's not only attainable, it's essential. As you delve deeper, you'll uncover actionable ways to fuse ancient wisdom with modern living, ensuring that the path of enlightenment remains accessible and relevant for all, no matter the era or circumstance.

Chapter 2:

Applying Buddhism in the Modern World

As we transition from the foundational tenets of Buddhism, this chapter serves as a bridge that connects ancient wisdom to our present-day challenges. How can millennia-old teachings provide solace, guidance, and tools in a world dominated by technology, relentless pace, and evolving moral landscapes?

From understanding the profound impact of Buddhist teachings on mental health to discerning the role of perception in managing stress, we will unearth the myriad ways Buddhism shines its light on our modern existence. As we explore practices like mindful eating, nature walks, and engaging with art, we're reminded that Buddhism isn't just about sitting in meditation—it's a holistic approach to life.

Whether you're searching for practical techniques or deeper philosophical insights, this chapter promises a journey that intertwines ancient Buddhist practices with the fabric of our contemporary lives.

Buddhist Wisdom on Mental Health

As we delve deeper into how to apply Buddhism in various facets of modern life, let us begin by addressing the cornerstone of well-being: mental health. It is no secret that a growing number of individuals are drawn to the wisdom of Buddhism, not necessarily for spiritual enlightenment but with the hope of finding solace and cognitive healing through its teachings. In a world brimming with complexities and challenges, the ancient yet timeless principles of Buddhism offer a sanctuary for the mind and a path toward inner peace.

The Role of Perception in Stress Management

Stress, as described in Buddhist teachings and backed by modern research, is deeply personal and rooted in one's perceptions and reactions to life's challenges. It's a manifestation of suffering stemming from numerous problems one encounters in the journey of life. The nuances of our emotional, mental, and experiential landscapes determine how we interpret the problems before us. If an individual perceives a problem as monumental and beyond their control, stress takes hold. On the contrary, viewing challenges as surmountable puzzles prevents the onset of stress.

This perspective resonates profoundly with the Buddhist idea that life, by its very nature, includes elements like aging, sickness, death, and separation from loved ones. Such unavoidable realities, along with external predicaments related to finances, work, societal expectations, and personal relationships, can all be sources of stress.

But what's even more enlightening is that often, the root of our stress doesn't lie in actual events but in our anticipation of them, in the fear of what might happen. We conjure images and scenarios that evoke feelings of worry, anxiety, fear, anger, and disappointment, and our brain, unable to differentiate between reality and imagined stressors, reacts as if the fictitious scenarios were real threats.

The Buddhist path offers tools to navigate this labyrinth of real and perceived problems. By mastering the art of calming the mind, one learns to regulate negative emotions and reactive feelings. Techniques like tranquility meditation allow one to achieve this calmness, and insight meditation helps develop wisdom, leading to a purified stress-free mind. A pivotal method used is the practice of breathing meditation (Ānāpānasati), which, when done with mindfulness and awareness, equips individuals to handle stressors with grace and poise (Channuwong et al., 2018).

In essence, the Buddhist approach to stress management isn't about evading problems but reshaping our perceptions and responses to them. By training the mind to approach challenges with understanding and clarity, we open the door to genuine mental peace.

Ethical Living: A Foundation for Mental Health

As we explore the roots of Buddhist teachings, we find that living by a moral code not only nurtures a harmonious society but also enhances individual well-being. Ethical actions and the practice of the Eightfold Path moral virtues such as "right speech" and "right action" foster mental strength and self-control, thereby reducing the chances of experiencing negative emotions such as guilt or regret, which can lead to perceived stress and even depression (Bergland, 2022).

Observing the Five Precepts

A remarkable study centered in Thailand demonstrated the positive effects of adhering to Buddhism's Five Precepts, a set of ethical guidelines that encourage individuals to follow the path of righteousness. The study found that individuals who observed these precepts reported experiencing less stress and fewer depressive symptoms (Wongpakaran et al., 2022).

The Five Precepts, or Pañca Sīla, are as follows:

1. Not killing any living creature.
2. Not stealing or taking what is not given.
3. Abstaining from false speech and avoiding divisive language and gossip.
4. Avoiding intoxicants that hinder clear thinking.
5. Abstaining from sexual misconduct or abuse.

Even if one does not identify as a Buddhist, embracing these virtues in a secular manner could be a path to avoiding life-altering mistakes and striving to foster positivity in your life—and the world—by making ethical choices. This approach also promotes mental strength and self-control, which subsequently buffers against mental health issues such as depression.

Beyond the Precepts: The Ten Paramitas

For those willing to take a step further, Buddhism also encourages the cultivation of the Ten Paramitas, or perfect virtues, which include attributes such as generosity, tolerance, truthfulness, and loving-kindness. Each Paramita invites us to cultivate a specific quality, enriching not only our own lives but also the lives of those around us through a ripple effect of positive actions and energies.

As we walk this path, we naturally foster a mind that is more resilient and less susceptible to stress and depression. When we nurture these virtues, we find ourselves better equipped to face the challenges that life throws at us. The cultivation of loving-kindness, for instance, can allow us to approach relationships with a warmer, more understanding heart, reducing conflicts and enhancing our connections with others. Likewise, nurturing truthfulness encourages us to live with integrity, which can foster a deeper sense of peace and self-respect.

In the journey of exploring and embracing these virtues, we create a nurturing ground for mental wellness, making us more resilient in navigating the waters of uncertainty and change. Moreover, it sets a strong foundation for ethical living, steering us toward actions that are in harmony with the greater good, and fostering a society rooted in understanding and mutual respect.

Buddhist Insights into Decision-Making

In a world saturated with options and information, it is easy to find ourselves overwhelmed when faced with decisions, big or small. This pervasive feeling is often termed "decision fatigue," a phenomenon where the quality of the decisions we make deteriorates after a long session of decision-making (Pignatiello et al., 2018). It's not just about choosing between significant life paths—sometimes even deciding what to have for dinner can seem like a mountainous task.

Buddhist teachings can serve as a breath of fresh air, offering us tools and virtues to navigate this labyrinth of choices with wisdom and serenity. By utilizing these teachings, we can craft a decision-making process that is not only wise and compassionate but also attuned to the intrinsic values of mindfulness and awareness.

At the heart of Buddhist decision-making is the application of mindfulness, where we pause to fully engage with the present moment; giving ourselves the space to respond rather than react impulsively. It encourages us to approach each decision with a calm and focused mind, sifting through options with careful consideration and a heart grounded in compassion and ethical values.

Similarly, the cultivation of virtues such as patience, understanding, and wisdom—embodied in the Ten Paramitas—serve as a beacon; guiding us in times of uncertainty. For instance, fostering generosity might guide us to make choices that prioritize communal well-being over individual gains, promoting a more harmonious society.

The Buddhist practice of mindfulness meditation can prove beneficial when combating decision fatigue. Through regular practice, we cultivate a mind that can discern the essential from the non-essential, fostering clarity and reducing the exhaustion that comes from constant decision-making. This practice empowers us to greet each choice with a fresh, clear mind, attuned to our inner wisdom and the nuances of each unique situation.

Moreover, Buddhist teachings emphasize the impermanent nature of all phenomena, reminding us that every decision, whether perceived as right or wrong, is not final but part of a continuously evolving process. This perspective can reduce the pressure often associated with decision-making, inviting a more flexible and forgiving approach where we learn and grow through the natural unfolding of life's journey.

By integrating the wisdom and virtues advocated in Buddhism into our decision-making process, we equip ourselves with a gentle yet potent shield against decision fatigue, creating a pathway toward choices that are more conscious, compassionate, and aligned with a deeper understanding of our interconnected existence.

In the upcoming chapter, we will delve deeper into the rich tapestry of Buddhist ethics, particularly exploring the Ten Paramitas. These teachings offer us a robust framework for understanding and navigating the complex ethical issues we encounter in today's fast-paced and ever-evolving world.

The Tools of Buddhism for Modern Challenges

While we have spoken—and will continue to speak—to the pivotal roles mindfulness and meditation play in navigating the modern world, it is time to clearly delineate the terms, their roles, the different types, and the various techniques associated with them. The techniques steeped in this philosophy are as applicable today as they were centuries ago, guiding individuals to harbor a sanctuary of peace amidst the chaos, a haven of clarity amidst the confusion.

Mindfulness: More than a Buzzword

In recent years, especially in the wake of the global pandemic, the term "mindfulness" has blossomed from a practice rooted in ancient Buddhist teachings to a buzzword resonating in the thoughts of wellness and mental health communities across the world. As the contemporary landscape shifts and molds to unprecedented challenges, individuals are turning to mindfulness as a source of refuge, a sanctuary of tranquility amidst the storms of unease that often assail our mental and emotional well-being.

At its core, mindfulness implies a conscious presence in the moment, guided by a gentle, non-judgmental regard for one's experiences, thoughts, and feelings. It involves a harmonious intertwining of the mind and body, rejecting the dualistic approach to understanding oneself and emphasizing a holistic, integrated perception of our existence (Anālayo, 2020).

Additionally, the rich tapestry of mindfulness involves various approaches and techniques tailored to different needs and circumstances. From practices that nurture an awareness of our bodily postures to methods directing focus toward our breath, mindfulness takes many forms, each offering a unique pathway to grounding oneself in the present moment.

In the early Buddhist discourses, a noteworthy approach to cultivating mindfulness is directing awareness to one's physical stances, a practice even undertaken by the Buddha-to-be in his quest for awakening. This form of mindfulness offers a potent tool for facing fears; fostering a grounded existence especially relevant in navigating the challenges posed by the pandemic (Anālayo, 2020).

Techniques for Incorporating Mindfulness into Daily Routines

To ease into the nurturing embrace of mindfulness, one can begin with small, yet consistent practices that foster a conscious presence in the daily commotion of life. Here are some practical tips and techniques to help you embark on this enriching journey (Monteiro, 2015):

Breath Awareness

- **Getting Started**: Find a quiet space where you can sit or lie down comfortably. Begin by taking deep and slow breaths, focusing your attention on the sensation of the air as it enters and leaves your nostrils.

- **Daily Integration**: You can practice breath awareness at different moments throughout your day, perhaps as you wake up in the morning, during breaks at work, or before you go to bed; fostering a calm start and end to your day.

Body Scan

- **Getting Started**: Commence with a comfortable posture, preferably lying down. Start from the tip of your toes and note any sensations, tensions, or relaxations without judgment as you slowly move your focus up your body, part by part, until you reach the crown of your head.

- **Daily Integration**: A body scan can be integrated into your bedtime routine to encourage relaxation and deeper sleep, helping to soothe away the physical stresses of the day.

Mindful Eating

- **Getting Started**: As you sit down for a meal, take a moment to appreciate the appearance and aroma of the food. As you eat, do so slowly, savoring each bite and paying attention to the textures and flavors in your mouth.

- **Daily Integration**: Try to have at least one mindful meal each day, where you eat without distractions like television or smartphones; fully engaging with the experience of nourishment.

Nature Walks

- **Getting Started**: Choose a path that is safe and surrounded by natural elements. As you walk, immerse yourself in the surroundings and pay careful attention to the sensations around you, such as the feeling of the terrain under your feet, the sounds of birds, the rustling leaves, and the fragrance of flowers and plants.

- **Daily Integration**: Consider carving out moments in your weekly or daily schedule to immerse yourself in nature walks, disconnected from the digital world and attuned to the vibrant life around you. It not only promotes mindfulness but also serves as a wonderful exercise for your physical well-being.

Reflective Journaling

- **Getting Started**: Equip yourself with a journal and a pen. Dedicate a quiet time in your day to note down your thoughts, feelings, and experiences without any judgment.

- **Daily Integration**: You might establish a routine of journaling either at the beginning or the end of your day, creating a space to reflect and be present with your inner world.

Community Engagement

- **Getting Started**: Begin by cultivating a conscious presence in your interactions with others. Listen actively, maintain eye contact, and respond with kindness and understanding.

- **Daily Integration**: In your daily interactions—be it with family, friends, or colleagues—try to be fully present; fostering a space of respect and mutual understanding based on Buddhist principles of ethics and community.

Engaging with Art and Stories

- **Getting Started**: Choose an art piece or a story and spend time contemplating it deeply, absorbing the details, the emotions it evokes, and the narratives it holds.

- **Daily Integration**: Integrate this practice into your leisure time, finding joy and deeper understanding through mindful engagement with the creative expressions of others.

As we delve deeper into the practice of mindfulness, we discover that it is indeed more than a contemporary buzzword—it is a timeless practice that holds the keys to unlocking a life filled with peace, joy, and grounded awareness; offering a nurturing embrace in the tumultuous seas of modern life.

The Transformative Journey through Buddhist Meditation

After embracing the nurturing realms of mindfulness, we pave our path deeper into the quiet, reflective avenues of meditation. A practice beyond mindfulness, a step further in our inward journey to finding peace and navigating the complexities of our inner world.

Mindfulness and meditation, while being overlapping concepts, stand as two pillars supporting our mental and emotional well-being. Mindfulness invites us to be fully present, welcoming each moment with open arms and a non-judgmental mind. Meditation takes this a notch higher, nudging us to delve deeper, to actively engage with our inner selves, and to achieve the personal development necessary for profound peace and well-being.

In a world where our perspectives are often tinted by craving or aversion, we can find ourselves imprisoned within a cycle of bitterness, desire, or discontent; losing sight of the world's true, interconnected essence. When we cultivate hearts brimming with generosity and kindness, a clear and beautiful vista unveils itself, revealing a world rich in beauty and interconnection.

Buddhist meditation embarks on this transformative journey, steering us away from the superficial distractions and chaos of the external world, and guiding us to the fertile grounds of our inner landscapes. Contrary to other forms of meditation that might involve hypnotic states or contacting supernatural entities, Buddhist meditation insists on a harmonious integration of body and mind, transcending the duality to regard them as a unified entity. It seeks not just peace, but a focused and heightened awareness that blossoms from controlled, still, and serene cognitive landscapes.

This meditative process is a rich tapestry woven with threads of various mental states such as calmness, concentration, and profound one-pointedness, which is fostered through the conscious nurturing of six powerful forces: Hearing, pondering, mindfulness, awareness, effort, and intimacy. These forces are the seeds we sow in the garden of our minds, a deliberate practice, far removed from passive engagement, where we foster ground for mindfulness to flourish.

Here in the tranquil arms of meditation, we embrace an environment conducive to healing, a nurturing space where

40

deep-seated fears and anxieties are not merely faced but held with gentleness, understood, and then released. The techniques applied offer not only personal solace but also avenues to connect with larger communities, reminding us of our intertwined existence with other beings, fostering a sense of unity, and grounding our comprehension of our position in the grand scheme.

Whether undertaken alone or within a group, perhaps in a retreat known as a sesshin or in a dedicated meditation room or zendo, this practice offers an enriching experience. Meditating with others stands as a poignant reminder of our place in a larger Buddhist community and in the vast interconnected community of beings encompassing every species.

Through Buddhist meditation, we are invited to a space where the mind refrains from aimless wanderings, reaching a state of peaceful focus; nurturing an aware, clear, and unified mind-body landscape; and fostering a beautiful inner sanctuary of peace, grounding, and interconnected awareness.

The Panorama of Buddhist Meditation

As you embark on this internal voyage, it is essential to find a meditation method that resonates with you. At its core, meditation is about being fully present, where the chatter of the mind stills, and you exist in a state of pure "being," untouched by judgment or disruptive thoughts.

Within the diverse realm of Buddhist meditation, you will discover a variety of meditation types and techniques derived from different Buddhist traditions that you can adopt in your daily life to foster inner peace and self-discovery.

For a deeper understanding, the insights on the types and methods outlined in this section have been drawn from a comprehensive BBC article on Buddhist meditation (BBC, 2009). I encourage you to refer to it as a reliable source to complement your learning journey.

Types of Meditation

Understanding the diversity of meditation practices can be facilitated by categorizing them into four primary types:

- **Concentrative**: This approach, used in techniques such as the Samatha meditation, is based on on calming and concentrating the mind by focusing on an object, sound, or sensation. Breath is a common focus, guiding you through varying stages of deepening awareness. Engage in exercises like "mindfulness of breathing," where you progress through stages of heightened awareness of your breath's sensation, leading to deeper absorption known as dhyana in Buddhism.

- **Generative**: This style fosters the development of loving kindness (metta bhavana) and compassion. It utilizes memory and imagination to cultivate a heart brimming with goodwill for oneself and others. It is a progressive practice with stages leading to universal love and kindness. An example is the Metta meditation technique. Here, we gradually expand our circle of love, starting from ourselves, extending to our loved ones and even our foes, and eventually embracing all beings in the warm hug of compassion.

- **Receptive**: This method emphasizes openness to experiences without judgment, fostering a receptive attitude toward arising sensations and experiences while encouraging the release of judgment and attachment. Practices like the Zen Buddhist zazen (or "just sitting") and the Tibetan tradition dzogchen embody this approach, encouraging undisturbed presence in the moment with unclouded eyes and an open heart, where you tenderly observe your thoughts and feelings as they emerge.

- **Reflective**: Techniques such as the Vipassana meditation exemplify this approach. It involves contemplative meditation where you continuously focus on a theme, promoting deep personal reflection and leading to deeper insights and understanding. It can include pondering on the teachings of Buddha, impermanence, and the interconnectedness of all things.

Classical Methods of Meditation

- **Breathing Meditation**: Central to many meditation practices is focusing on one's breath. This involves sitting calmly and immersing in the natural rhythms of your breath, without actively altering it or being encumbered by notions of right or wrong. You are encouraged to count breaths up to ten, returning to one if distractions arise, and progressively deepen your focus on the breathing process.

- **Walking Meditation**: A popular practice in Zen Buddhism, walking meditation seamlessly blends mindfulness and movement. It allows you to meditate while walking, bringing awareness to each step, the sensations of the earth beneath you, and the rhythm of your breath, which nurtures a sense of groundedness and peace.

- **Visual Concentration**: Some practices involve focusing on an object like a candle flame or a flower, offering an external focal point to guide your meditative process.

Mindfulness and Zen Meditation

As we learned, mindfulness is interconnected with meditation but stands slightly apart. It emphasizes becoming fully aware of one's experiences in all aspects of life. In Zen—a prominent branch in the panorama of Buddhist meditation—this is practiced by being wholly absorbed in the moment, undistracted by thoughts, fears, or hopes, hence experiencing each moment directly. It encourages the practice of "just being," where you strive to engage wholly in every activity, disentangling yourself from the distractions of thoughts, fears, and hopes.

Mindfulness, coupled with self-discipline cultivated through persevering with meditation despite discomfort or boredom, invites you to a deeper engagement with each moment, offering a pathway to liberation from the mind's unrest and a plain view into the vast landscape of the present moment.

- **Zazen**: Central to Zen, this method involves sitting in a quiet space, connecting deeply with the present moment, understanding the true nature of reality, and thus achieving a harmonized state of mind. The practice emphasizes a variety of postures but universally encourages maintaining a straight spine to foster focused meditation.

- **Koan Meditation**: This technique employs paradoxical questions or statements, known as koans, to foster spiritual understanding and provoke enlightenment. A traditional example is the "What is the sound of one hand clapping?" question. Koans serve as a powerful tool in guiding practitioners to deeper levels of insight.

The Three Trainings

For many embarking on a spiritual journey in the West, meditation is often their first encounter. However, in the Buddhist framework, meditation is the second element of the "Threefold Path." Before meditation comes ethics, also known as the path of morality, establishes the foundation for righteous living. It emphasizes the importance of living a life that abstains from causing harm to oneself and others.

This ethical grounding paves the way for effective meditation. Meditation serves as a tool to develop clarity and concentration in the mind, setting a path for the final training: The cultivation of wisdom, an exploration into the true nature of life and experiences.

Incorporating Meditation into Daily Routines

Through the practice of meditation methods and types, you are not just developing self-discipline but gradually learning to still the mind, overcome distractions, and delve deeper into the truth of your being, nurturing a sense of peace and connection to the universe. It is a journey toward freeing the mind from its restless wanderings and glimpsing the expansive, vibrant moment present here and now.

Preparation and Posture

In traditional Buddhist practices, the "lotus position" is the classic meditation posture. This means sitting cross-legged with each foot resting on the opposite thigh. But let's be honest, this isn't feasible for everyone. If the lotus position seems challenging or isn't convenient for the time and place, don't fret.

Simply sitting on the floor, whether kneeling or cross-legged, ensuring both knees touch the ground with an erect back can be equally effective. If you're not a fan of sitting on the floor, a chair works too. What matters is maintaining a posture that keeps your spine straight, supporting your alert yet relaxed state.

And let's not forget the revered practice of walking meditation—also a cornerstone in the Buddhist tradition. This practice extends beyond the confinements of a designated meditation space and can be integrated into daily routines, be it while walking in a park, moving in your living space, or even during brief strolls at work. It's a gentle reminder that meditation is not limited to sitting in stillness—it is about fostering mindfulness in every facet of our lives; turning ordinary actions into moments of deep connection and presence.

Remember, while posture aids meditation, the true essence of this practice is the inner journey of the mind. Begin and end each meditation session by tuning into your feelings and bodily sensations, allowing thoughts to naturally ebb and flow, and therefore grounding yourself in the present.

Embarking on the Meditation Path

Over the decades, meditation has beautifully integrated itself into Western practices. Similar to how hatha yoga and T'ai Chi have been embraced for their wellness benefits, Buddhist meditation has carved its space, although it is not often necessarily linked to religious beliefs. From managing stress and developing concentration to assisting in palliative care, such as managing chronic pain or preventing depression relapse, it can provide a multitude of benefits.

And while the practice has gained immense popularity with numerous resources available, the universal suggestion remains:

Meditating in a community and under the guidance of experienced teachers often provides a richer experience.

So, it's not just about individual practice. Participating in group retreats can intensify the focus on meditation, offering a sanctuary to dive deeper, with fellow practitioners sharing the same journey. But this is not a rule.

As you embrace these practices, remember to choose a method that not only resonates with you but also establishes depth and a personal connection in your meditative journey. It doesn't matter if you prefer to sit silently, chant mantras, or walk mindfully, the essence is to find your unique path in the rich panorama of Buddhist meditation.

In your daily life, you can practice these meditative methods in a space of stillness, be it facing a wall as in the Soto tradition or sitting in a circle as in the Rinzai tradition. Whether alone or in a group, the key is to create a harmonious rhythm of practice. This embodies the core Buddhist principle of mindful living, which involves having an open heart and a still mind that's ready to embrace the beauty and depth of each moment in its fullness.

As we venture into this fulfilling journey, let us equip ourselves with practical strategies to meditate effectively. Dr. Bhante Saranapala, a modern sage, will guide us through these processes with enriching insights (Mahabir, 2019):

1. **Comfortable Posture**: Choose an inviting and quiet space where you can sit with an upright, yet relaxed posture. Let your hands rest on your lap, and gently close your eyes, inviting calmness.

2. **Breath Awareness**: Focus on your breath, feeling the natural rhythm as you inhale and exhale. If your mind wanders, gently bring it back to the breath, nurturing a harmonious breath-mind relationship.

3. **Facing Your Inner Pain**: During meditation, you might encounter pain and fear surfacing from within. Recognize them without resistance, acknowledge their presence, and offer them kindness and understanding.

4. **Shining Light on Negative Thoughts**: When negative thoughts arise, welcome them with awareness, observe without judgment, and slowly let them go, embracing the light of mindfulness that fosters healing and peace.

5. **Consistency is Key**: Foster a regular meditation practice, starting with just 15 minutes a day, and gradually increasing the duration as you build your "mental fitness" over time.

With these practical guides and techniques to show you the way, we invite you to embark on a meditative journey; a path of inner exploration and healing. As Dr. Saranapala articulates, meditation is akin to "internal medicine" for peace and well-being; a nourishing practice that empowers us to face our inner fears and cultivate a sanctuary of peace within ourselves, gradually blossoming into individuals embodying kindness, compassion, and undying joy (Mahabir, 2019).

Remember, this chapter has merely opened the door to showcase how Buddhism offers invaluable insights into managing contemporary challenges, from mental health to the labyrinth of decision-making.

Yet, our journey is only beginning. As we progress, the next chapter will provide a profound dive into Buddhism and ethics—a cornerstone of the three trainings and the very essence of a Buddhist way of life.

In subsequent chapters, anticipate explorations on how these teachings illuminate our path in areas like relationships, technology, environmental stewardship, community building, and crafting one's personal spiritual journey. So, as we turn the page together, may your heart and mind be open, ready to absorb, reflect, and apply the timeless wisdom of Buddhism in this ever-evolving world.

Chapter 3:

Buddhism and Ethics

In the previous chapter, we familiarized ourselves with the transformative world of meditation, an integral part of the threefold training outlined by Buddha to foster spiritual development and well-being. In recapitulating, we grounded ourselves in the understanding that meditation, rich in its ability to nurture clarity and focus, finds its rooting in the preceding path of morality, known as "sīla." This paves the way for wisdom, the final element in the threefold path.

Now, as we move forward, we focus on exploring the basic ideas of Buddhist ethics that lay the foundation of sīla. Buddha's teachings show us that sīla isn't just about following a strict set of rules or moral duties. It's an invitation to a happier and more peaceful life where we live naturally in a way that promotes goodness and avoids harm. It guides us to foster a mindset that is aware and pure, transforming rules into a joyful way of life built on understanding and compassion.

The pivotal journey through sīla is closely intertwined with mindfulness and intention. Just as with any other part of the Buddhist path, the underlying intention behind one's actions holds a paramount place when it comes to the precepts. This, however, doesn't give leeway to justify misconduct through ignorance or inattention.

Engaging deeply with this ethical foundation requires a vigilant mind, continually attuned to the currents of thought and action, nurturing an environment where wholesome desires flourish and unwholesome appeals diminish. This purification process is not only conducive to deep meditation but also the cultivation of wisdom, where one begins to comprehend the mutable and interconnected nature of all phenomena (Buddho.org, n.d.).

In this chapter, we will delve deeper into the nurturing grounds of sīla and its core principles, aiming to explore how this Buddhist approach to ethics not only fosters respect for oneself and others but can also offer solutions to certain modern ethical dilemmas. Through the practice of sīla, we learn to embrace a lifestyle steeped in kindness and compassion, expanding our understanding of the complex web of cause and effect that governs all phenomena.

Central to this exploration is the profound principle of karma, a concept deeply woven into the fabric of the cosmos that represents the intrinsic laws of moral causality. In Buddhist teaching, karma dictates that our intentional actions inherently possess the potential to breed consequences that mirror the moral quality of the actions undertaken.

This recognition of karma as governing cosmic law, amidst other systems such as the laws of consciousness and spiritual development, offers a deeper lens to view our actions and their repercussions, emphasizing that a fulfilling life is woven through a series of ethical choices grounded in understanding and compassion.

Through this lens, we invite you to explore the depth of sīla, a practice fostering inner peace and a harmonious society, working hand in hand with the universal laws of karma to craft a life of purpose, understanding, and mindful living.

The Five Precepts: A Guideline for Conscious Living

Our exploration of the moral fabric of Buddhism brings us to the nurturing teachings of the Buddha, a guide grounded in the Five Precepts or pañca-sīla, which translates to the five virtues. These are represented as a set of guidelines rather than commandments, and they encourage moral and ethical behavior in everyday life. They serve as a practical guide, encouraging individuals to live with awareness and compassion.

These precepts, fundamentally connected to the Eightfold Path's Right Action, Right Speech, and Right Livelihood, invite us to:

1. Abstain from taking life.
2. Abstain from taking what is not given.
3. Abstain from sexual misconduct.
4. Abstain from false speech.
5. Abstain from intoxicating substances leading to heedlessness.

In our previous discussion, we touched upon a study highlighting how observing the Five Precepts could potentially reduce stress and depressive symptoms in individuals (Wongpakaran et al., 2022). In this chapter, we delve deeper into each precept, offering a modern interpretation to help you integrate these timeless teachings into your contemporary life. Our exploration will be grounded in insights drawn from an insightful article on Buddho.org (n.d. -a).

First Precept: Abstain from Killing

At its core, abstaining from killing revolves around fostering a deep reverence and respect for all forms of life. It is one of the fundamental precepts in Buddhism that encourages individuals to live harmoniously with all beings, appreciating the sanctity of life that pervades every creature, big or small.

In the modern context, this teaching can find application at both physical and mental levels:

- **Physically**: Adopt a conscious approach to your daily activities. For instance, be aware of your surroundings to avoid accidentally harming smaller beings. Taking it a step further, one could explore dietary choices that are aligned with non-harm, such as vegetarianism or veganism, which strive to cause lesser harm to animals and the environment.

- **Mentally**: Nourishing a gentle and loving mindset goes beyond physical action. It is about curbing hostile and malicious thoughts and fostering mettā, a loving-kindness perspective toward all beings. The practice of mettā meditation could be a practical way to cultivate such a mindset, where you visualize sending love and kindness to all beings and gradually expand your circle of compassion.

Imagine a day when you consciously decide to walk with awareness. As you stroll through a garden, your eyes catch a line of ants marching across the path. Instead of continuing forward, indifferent to their existence, you take a thoughtful detour to avoid disturbing their path.

As your day progresses, you apply this principle in interactions with others, choosing understanding over anger and kindness over irritation. It even translates to your internal thoughts, offering yourself compassion instead of criticism. You embrace the realization that you are not intrinsically superior to any other being, not even within your species, fostering a deep-seated respect for all life forms.

As we mentioned, vegetarianism and veganism can be paths to cause less harm to animals and be kinder to our environment, but it is important to recognize the complex web of life in which we exist. Human beings, being a part of the natural order, are essentially omnivorous. In this light, the act of consuming meat can be viewed not necessarily as a breach of ethical conduct but as a part of the natural cycle, as long as it is carried out with a consciousness of sustainability and respect for the life that is being sacrificed to nourish another.

It's a delicate balance, where understanding the interconnectedness of all beings and respecting the circle of life become vital in nurturing an ethical perspective that is both compassionate and grounded in the realities of our biological nature. Thus, even in the complexity of our choices, the guidance is to lean toward kindness, understanding, and a deep reverence for all life.

To embody this precept in your daily life, try to cultivate awareness through simple exercises:

- **Mindful Walking**: When walking, be fully present and notice the small creatures that cross your path, allowing them the space and respect they deserve.

- **Mettā Meditation**: Dedicate a few minutes each day to practice mettā meditation. Start with yourself, then gradually extend your wishes of well-being and happiness to family, friends, and eventually to all beings.

- **Reflection**: At the end of the day, reflect on your actions and thoughts. Celebrate your successes in adhering to this precept and acknowledge areas where you can improve, fostering a mindset of continuous growth and learning.

When you integrate this mindful approach to life you not only abstain from harming others but also create a peaceful sanctuary within yourself, a refuge of loving-kindness and respect for all life. Remember, it's a journey of small steps, with every act of kindness serving as a seed planted that nurtures a garden of compassion and harmony with all forms of life.

Second Precept: Abstain from Stealing

Abstaining from stealing, the second precept in Buddhism, invites us to foster respect and consideration for others by honoring their boundaries, possessions, and time. This precept goes deeper than not engaging in theft; it is about nurturing a heart that respects what belongs to others, including the environment.

In today's fast-paced society, understanding and living by this precept can be a grounding practice, reminding us to live ethically and harmoniously with others. It finds resonance at various levels:

- **Physically**: Cultivate respect for the belongings of others, going beyond just physical possessions to include respecting others' boundaries, time, and energy. Avoid taking anything that is not freely given, including small things that might sometimes be overlooked, such as office supplies or a piece of gum.

- **Mentally**: To counteract tendencies to covet what belongs to others, nurture a spirit of generosity, or dāna. This includes not only sharing material goods but also offering kindness, understanding, and help to those around you, hence fostering a supportive and giving community.

Imagine you are at work and notice a colleague engrossed in a task with a tight deadline. Recognizing the importance of respecting their time, you decide to hold off on sharing a casual story and instead offer a word of encouragement or a helping hand, showing both respect for their time and a generous spirit. This is a simple yet practical way to embody the ethos of not taking what is not given freely and extending space and understanding instead.

Similarly, in the digital space where instant messaging reigns, it's easy to expect immediate responses from friends and acquaintances when we reach out. However, it is crucial to practice patience and respect toward others' timelines and emotional states.

Even if it seems like someone has the time to respond to your message, they might be dealing with other priorities or simply not be in the right mindset to engage at that moment. By giving them the space to respond in their own time, you adhere to the respectful practice of not demanding what isn't offered willingly, fostering understanding and empathy in your online interactions.

To integrate this precept into your daily life, you might consider the following exercises:

- **Mindful Communication**: Before engaging someone in a conversation, take a moment to assess if it's the right time. Offering your presence and listening without imposing can also be a generous act.

- **Generosity Practice**: Challenge yourself to perform small acts of generosity daily. It could be as simple as sharing a smile, giving a compliment, or helping someone in need.

- **Reflection**: Reflect daily on your actions and thoughts to recognize and appreciate your efforts to respect others' boundaries and foster a spirit of generosity, kindness, and mutual respect, be it online or offline.

If you embrace the spirit of this precept, you pave the way for a society rooted in respect, understanding, and generosity where everyone's boundaries are honored, and the spirit of giving is celebrated. It's about building a culture that cherishes harmonious relationships and nurtures a sense of communal well-being and trust.

Third Precept: Abstain from Sexual Misconduct

Rooted in the wisdom of Buddhism is the counsel to abstain from sexual misconduct, a teaching that holds relevance not only in romantic relationships but in all interpersonal connections. This precept encourages individuals to foster relationships grounded in respect, consent, and mutual understanding, creating a foundation for harmonious interactions.

In the modern setting, this precept offers a beacon of light to guide individuals in forming and nurturing relationships that are safe, respectful, and consensual. It resonates on different levels:

- **Physically**: Ensure that all relationships, especially those that involve sexual intimacy, are grounded in mutual consent and understanding. This means being attentive to the feelings and wishes of others and always respecting their boundaries and choices.

- **Mentally**: Foster a mental environment that respects the autonomy and dignity of others. This involves cultivating loyalty, honesty, and empathy in relationships, ensuring that your mind harbors no intentions that could harm or distress others.

Consider a scenario where a couple is navigating the early stages of their relationship. By engaging in open and transparent communication, they openly discuss their boundaries, desires, and expectations. They ensure to check in with each other regularly, valuing mutual understanding and respect over personal gratification. This conscious effort to maintain a relationship grounded in mutual respect is a living embodiment of abstaining from sexual misconduct.

To embed the essence of this precept in daily life, you might contemplate these actionable tips:

- **Self-Reflection**: Regularly take time to reflect on your actions and intentions in relationships, encouraging a mindset that honors the dignity and choices of others.

- **Open Dialogue**: Create spaces for open dialogue in relationships, where each individual feels safe to express their needs, fears, and boundaries without judgment.

- **Education**: Continuously educate yourself on the principles of consent and respectful relationships, nurturing an understanding that promotes well-being for all involved.

By harmoniously uniting this ancient wisdom with contemporary understanding, individuals can foster relationships that are not just respectful and consensual but deeply nurturing and enriching. This precept thus serves as a pathway to relationships that are healthy, respectful, and grounded in the deep appreciation of each other's inherent worth.

Fourth Precept: Abstain from Wrong Speech

In the intricate tapestry of Buddhist teachings, the principle of abstaining from wrong speech stands as a vital thread, guiding individuals to communicate with integrity, kindness, and mindfulness. This precept encourages us to create a space where harmony, truth, and respect flourish through mindful speech.

Words can sometimes be used carelessly in today's fast-paced, digital world leading to misunderstandings, hurt, and divisions. This is why the precept of avoiding wrong speech is more pertinent now than ever. Let us delve deeper into how this can be practically integrated into daily living:

- **Physically**: This involves consciously steering clear of gossip, misleading statements, and divisive speech that can sow discord in communities. It urges individuals to choose words that are truthful and promote harmony, thus fostering a more compassionate and understanding environment.

- **Mentally**: On a mental plane, this precept encourages the cultivation of a mindset that respects the truth and the maintenance of harmony in relationships. It nudges us to reflect before speaking, weigh the potential impact of our words on others, and choose a path of kindness and truthfulness at all times.

Imagine finding yourself amidst a group of friends where the conversation has veered toward gossip or discussing someone in a negative light. Choosing not to participate in the gossip and instead gently guiding the conversation toward a more uplifting and inclusive topic reflects adherence to this precept. It can be as simple as sharing a positive story or discussing common interests that unite rather than divide.

To embody this principle in your life, consider the following tips:

- **Mindful Listening**: Before responding to any conversation, take a moment to listen mindfully to the other person, fostering a dialogue grounded in understanding and respect.

- **Pause and Reflect**: Take a moment to reflect before responding, especially to argumentative statements, so you can allow space to choose words that are kind, truthful, and conducive to harmony.

- **Positive Affirmations**: Cultivate a habit of speaking positive affirmations to yourself, nurturing a mind that naturally gravitates toward truthful and harmonious speech.

This teaching allows us to forge connections that are deeper and more meaningful, fostering a society rooted in understanding, respect, and mutual appreciation. Through conscious communication, it is possible to build a world where speech becomes a bridge to understanding and a beacon of kindness and truth. It stands as a testament to the transformative power of words used wisely, nurturing hearts, and fostering unity through kind, respectful, and honest communication.

Fifth Precept: Abstain from the Use of Intoxicating Substances that Cause Inattention

Within the framework of Buddhist teachings, the call to abstain from consuming substances that induce heedlessness echoes the broader theme of mindful living—a life characterized by awareness, clarity, and thoughtful choices. This principle urges us to foster a lifestyle where our minds are unclouded, facilitating ethical living and deep self-awareness.

In a modern context, with an abundance of substances and distractions readily available, this precept is a gentle reminder to nurture a space of mindfulness within ourselves. Here's how this can be reflected in our day-to-day lives:

- **Physically**: This aspect focuses on avoiding overindulgence in substances that cloud our judgment and diminish our capacity for mindful living. It encourages moderation and thoughtful consumption to preserve the clarity of mind and body.

- **Mentally**: Beyond physical abstention, this principle invites us to foster a mental landscape rooted in mindfulness and moral rectitude. It is a commitment to remain present, to approach each moment with a clear and open mind, ready to embrace experiences with full awareness.

Picture yourself at a lively gathering where the use of recreational drugs and excessive alcohol consumption seems to be the norm. Rather than getting swept up in the fervor, you ground yourself in mindfulness and restraint and choose to avoid substances that could cloud your judgment and lead to inattention.

This decision not only safeguards your well-being but also allows you to maintain a level of conscious presence, capable of nurturing genuine connections and perhaps providing a steadying influence in an environment of potential excess. Through this choice, you become a beacon of self-respect and conscientious living, setting a kind and thoughtful example for others.

However, this precept, which advises against using intoxicants that lead to heedlessness, can be extended to include the mindless consumption of material goods. In a world where consumerism is rampant, applying mindfulness and discernment in our buying choices has become an increasingly important aspect of this precept. Being thoughtful about what we acquire encourages us to prioritize needs over wants, and to value the quality and longevity of goods over the instant gratification derived from impulsive purchases.

This principle nudges us to respect the resources and labor that go into producing these items, promoting a sense of gratitude and sufficiency that aligns well with Buddhist principles. It's a balanced approach that recognizes the middle path—avoiding extremes and encouraging moderation and mindfulness in all aspects of life.

To infuse your life with the essence of this teaching, you might want to consider the following:

- **Mindful Consumption**: Make a conscious choice regarding what you consume, be it food, drink, material goods, or media. Aim for choices that foster clarity and well-being, promoting a balanced and harmonious life.

- **"Low Profile" Strategy**: Consider adopting a "low profile" strategy by limiting your engagement with social media platforms and nurturing a space of personal reflection and presence in the real world.

- **Daily Meditation**: Establish a daily meditation practice to enhance mindfulness and foster a clear mind, providing a solid foundation for ethical living.

- **Reflective Journaling**: Maintain a journal to note down your experiences with mindfulness, helping you to be more attentive and present in your daily life.

If you embrace this principle, you walk a path grounded in awareness and intentionality, nurture a life rich with moments fully lived and appreciated, and promote a beautiful dance of mindful living where every step is taken with consciousness and joy. It is a journey toward a harmonious life, where the mind is unclouded and ready to embrace the beauty of the present moment in all its vividness and depth.

As we navigate through the intricacies of the Five Precepts, it is pivotal to remember that these guiding principles are not rigid prohibitions, but nurturing reminders encouraging us to walk a path of moderation and balance. The journey through the Five Precepts is not one of constraint but of liberation.

The Buddha, with his boundless wisdom, offered these precepts as gentle beacons to guide us away from extremes and toward a middle path, a journey characterized by mindfulness, compassion, and harmonious living. They serve as instruments that help us tune into a frequency of life that cherishes respect, understanding, and kindness, fostering environments where peace and harmony flourish.

Moreover, they guide us in crafting a life that is not just about refraining from negative actions but actively engaging in positive behaviors that nurture our growth and well-being. They encourage us to be mindful of our actions, to foster relationships grounded in respect and understanding, and to create a space within us that is a haven of peace, reverence for life, and mindfulness.

The Ten Paramis

As we journey deeper into the teachings of Buddhism, it's essential to understand that while the Five Precepts lay the foundation for moral and ethical living, another set of teachings guides us toward perfecting specific virtues. Just like the rings of a tree extend outward, encompassing more as they grow, the teachings expand, embracing the Five Precepts and the Ten Paramis and potentially overlapping in their guidance toward a moral and harmonious life.

As we touched upon earlier, these virtues are known as the Paramitas, or "perfections." The Ten Paramitas represent core qualities that every practitioner is encouraged to cultivate, leading to profound personal transformation and, eventually, enlightenment.

While harmonizing fundamentally with the precepts established in the Noble Eightfold Path, this parallel pathway places a focus on perfecting specific virtues, also referred to as Paramis in the Southern tradition and Paramitas in the Eastern and Northern traditions, thereby nurturing the individual into a figure of wholeness and enlightened understanding (The Buddhist Society, n.d.).

Though articulated slightly differently in these traditions, the essence remains strikingly congruent, underscoring the universal resonance of these virtues in guiding individuals toward a wholesome existence. In the Southern tradition, emphasis is laid on qualities such as renunciation, truthfulness, and equanimity, urging individuals to carve out a path of ethical living and cultivate compassion for themselves and others. According to the Southern tradition, the Ten Paramis include:

1. Generosity
2. Morality
3. Renunciation
4. Wisdom
5. Energy
6. Patience
7. Truthfulness
8. Determination
9. Loving-kindness
10. Equanimity

The Eastern and Northern traditions, on the other hand, introduce facets of meditation, skillful means, and knowledge, bringing to light the rich tapestry of personal development and evoking a deep understanding of life and the world.

They list the Ten Paramitas as follows:

1. Generosity
2. Morality
3. Patience
4. Energy
5. Meditation
6. Wisdom
7. Skillful means
8. Resolution
9. Power
10. Knowledge

It's remarkable to note the subtle nuances yet deep-seated alignment between the two interpretations, highlighting the adaptive and inclusive nature of Buddhist teachings and accommodating diverse pathways to attain enlightenment.

As we forge ahead in our exploration, we will anchor our focus on the Southern traditions, allowing us to delve deeper into each virtue and grasp its modern-day relevance and application.

Each of these Paramis, or perfections, furnishes us with tools to foster a life characterized by depth, understanding, and a joyous embrace of the inherent beauty found in ethical and mindful living.

These perfections foster a journey of introspection, aligning one's life with virtues that are intrinsically beautiful and conducive to well-being and inviting an exploratory pathway that is both enriching and nurturing.

First Paramis: Generosity (Dāna)

This principle calls us to foster a mindset that goes well beyond simple acts of charity. It encourages us to generously share with others without expecting something in return. This kind of generosity isn't confined to sharing material possessions; it extends to offering your time, sharing your knowledge, and expressing kindness in your daily interactions.

In a society where the emphasis is often heavily placed on personal gain, championing generosity stands as a beacon of hope, nurturing stronger and more connected communities. It operates on the simple yet powerful premise of caring for each other, breaking down barriers, and facilitating meaningful connections between individuals.

Putting this virtue into practice doesn't always require grand gestures; it can be seamlessly woven into the fabric of our daily lives. It could mean setting aside a small part of your earnings for a cause you believe in, volunteering your time for community service, or simply being available to lend a listening ear to a friend or a family member.

It encourages us to recognize and seize the little opportunities life presents us each day to extend kindness, fostering a circle of goodwill that echoes far and wide. Embracing a generous spirit nurtures a harmonious society where small acts of kindness are not the exception, but the norm. It creates a ripple effect, where each act of goodwill inspires another and paves the way for a kinder, warmer world for all.

Second Paramis: Morality (Sīla)

As touched upon earlier, embodying ethical and kind living serves as the heart of Buddhist philosophy. This principle guides us to engage in actions, speech, and thoughts that are grounded in kindness, advocating a pacifist approach in our interactions with others and the environment that avoids harmful practices.

In a world intricately connected through technology, every action we undertake has the potential to reverberate globally, transcending geographical barriers and impacting both individuals and the natural world in wider circles. It's therefore essential that we navigate this global landscape with a conscious awareness of the broader repercussions of our actions.

To cultivate a mindful approach to morality, we can initiate small yet significant changes in our day-to-day lives. Take a pause amidst your bustling routine to ponder the long-term impacts of your actions. Whether it is the choices you make while shopping, the way you communicate online, or the relationships you nurture; every action carves out a path in the grand tapestry of our interconnected society.

Encourage yourself to be consciously reflective as you decide how you will positively and meaningfully impact this world we live in. Aspire to be a source of goodness and understanding, and brainstorm ways to infuse this heightened awareness into your daily engagements.

By doing so, you foster a ripple effect of compassion and understanding, fostering a global community grounded in respect and mutual care. This conscious way of living not only enriches your personal journey but meaningfully contributes to a more harmonious world.

Third Paramis: Renunciation (Nekkhamma)

This virtue inspires us to consciously step away from our relentless pursuit of worldly pleasures and material attachments, encouraging us to appreciate the transient nature of all things physical. It nudges us to shift our focus from incessant wanting and instead turn to embracing simplicity and mindfulness by cultivating a deep-seated contentment that comes from within.

In a society that often equates happiness with material accumulation, the practice of renunciation emerges as a breath of fresh air, offering a novel perspective. It assists us in distinguishing between our true "needs," which are essential for our well-being, and our "wants," which are often driven by external influences and can lead to a never-ending cycle of desire and dissatisfaction.

Through renunciation, we cultivate a life of simplicity and contentment, finding joy in the present moment and in the non-materialistic aspects of life which are more fulfilling and sustainable.

To embody this Paramis in your daily life, initiate a routine of digital detox, perhaps dedicating a day each week to unplug from the digital world. During this time, encourage yourself to engage with nature, delve into a good book, meditate, or simply be present with your thoughts and feelings, fostering a deeper connection with your inner self.

This practice isn't about deprivation, but about creating space to connect with the aspects of life that are truly enriching and nurturing. It is about stepping back to forge a deeper connection with ourselves and the world around us in a more authentic and meaningful way.

Fourth Paramis: Wisdom (Pañña)

Our journey through the Ten Paramis has led us to the virtue of wisdom. This virtue nudges us to cultivate a good understanding of life and the world, steering us toward a path of greater understanding and insight. It invites us to go beyond surface-level perceptions and delve deeper to discern the true nature of things, thus living a life rich in depth and insight.

In today's fast-paced, technologically driven society, we are constantly bombarded with a deluge of information, some accurate, and some not. Here, the practice of wisdom becomes our ally, equipping us with the discernment to sift through this sea of information to discern what holds truth and what doesn't, thereby grounding our perspectives in reality rather than illusion. It encourages a mindful consumption of information and promotes a deeper understanding of the world that is both informed and nuanced.

To nurture this wisdom in your daily life, dedicate time regularly to contemplative activities that foster inner clarity and understanding, such as deep reading or meditation. Make a conscious effort to seek out reliable and reputable sources when consuming information, be it scientific articles, news, or other educational content. Consider setting aside a quiet time for reflection where you can ponder over what you've learned, encouraging a habit of critical thinking that seeks to understand the intricate dance of cause and effect in the world, and how you fit into this grand tapestry.

Fifth Paramis: Energy (Viriya)

As we explore the next Paramis, we turn our focus to "Viriya," which translates to a kind of diligent energy, a force that drives us to exert persistent effort and showcase resilience, even when faced with challenges. It's about harnessing a kind of strength that helps us persevere, fostering a spirit that does not easily bow down to failures but forges ahead with a hopeful heart and determined mind.

The modern world often offers us shortcuts, instant gratification, quick fixes, or immediate rewards, which can sometimes make the journey toward long-term goals seem laborious and taxing. Here, energy comes into play, encouraging us to persist with effort and patience and to nurture dreams that are deeper and more sustaining than fleeting pleasures.

To integrate energy into your life, start with setting clear, long-term goals for various aspects of your life. They could be related to your physical health, personal dreams, family well-being, or any other sphere that holds significance for you. Once these goals are set, break them down into smaller, manageable tasks, creating a roadmap toward your destination.

And as you reach each milestone, take a moment to acknowledge and celebrate your progress. This not only fosters a sense of accomplishment but also fuels your energy to press forward, embracing both the small and big victories with joy and gratitude and forging a path of purposeful living with diligence and joyous effort.

Sixth Paramis: Patience (Khanti)

Patience refers to the admirable ability to endure life's ups and downs with a graceful heart and a steady mind. This Paramis revolves around harboring a kind of patience that transcends the act of simply waiting by doing so with a compassionate understanding of the transitory nature of situations.

We often find ourselves rushing through life as we pursue deadlines and constantly race against time. It's during these chaotic moments that the principle of Khanti encourages us to pause, breathe, and adopt a stance of calm acceptance. This not only aids in reducing stress but also in maintaining a harmonious balance in our lives amidst external chaos. By accepting that not everything can be achieved instantly and that our grandiose goals require time and nurturing, we foster a tranquility that stands tall in the face of adversity.

To integrate patience into your daily life, make it a habit to pause and breathe deeply when confronted with stressful situations or irritants. In that quiet space, remind yourself of the transient nature of the circumstances and that achieving your meaningful goals will indeed take time.

Sometimes it helps to visualize the broader picture of life, seeing the current irritant as a small dot in the grand canvas that encompasses our world. Developing this perspective can be a calming force that facilitates well-balanced and peaceful living by guiding you to approach situations with a patient and understanding heart. It's like reassuring oneself that this too shall pass, and allowing that understanding to shape our reactions, nurturing a sanctuary of calm within ourselves amidst the storm.

Seventh Paramis: Truthfulness (Sacca)

Truthfulness is about nurturing honesty and integrity in all we say and do. Remember the Fourth Precept, which describes abstaining from wrong speech? This virtue urges us to be steadfast in speaking the truth, fostering a transparent approach in our interactions with others.

By choosing to be truthful, we not only uphold our integrity but also foster trust and build stronger bonds in both personal and professional spheres. Honest living goes beyond just speaking the truth; it extends to being genuine in our actions and thereby creating an environment of reliability and trustworthiness.

To cultivate truthfulness in your daily life, engage in the practice of mindful speech. Before expressing yourself, take a moment to reflect on your words. Ask yourself if what you're about to say is true, necessary, and kind. This simple reflection can help in avoiding needless conflicts and promotes understanding and harmonious relationships.

Imagine a space where words become the bridges to deeper connections, nurturing relationships that are grounded in truth and kindness. Start with small steps, perhaps by being more conscious of your daily conversations, and gradually, you will notice a change; a blossoming of more genuine and heartfelt interactions in your life.

Eighth Paramis: Determination (Adhiṭṭhāna)

Determination invites us to harbor an unwavering commitment to our journey, helping us stand firm amidst life's inevitable challenges and distractions. It nurtures resilience within us and encourages us to persevere in the face of obstacles that test our resolve; fostering a mindset of growth and boundless possibilities.

In today's digital age, where distractions are just a click away, maintaining a sense of determination is more crucial than ever. It isn't just about pursuing our goals with vigor—it is about staying true to our core values and life's purpose, ensuring we navigate our lives with a sense of intention and focus.

To foster determination in your daily life, try creating a vision board that encapsulates your aspirations and the values that are dear to you. Use this visual tool as a daily reminder of your path, a sort of roadmap to your authentic self; keeping you grounded and focused amidst the noise and demands of modern life. It could contain pictures, quotes, or any representation of your dreams and the kind of person you aspire to be.

As you review it regularly, allow yourself to reconnect with your intentions, diving deeper into your resolve to walk your path with steadfastness and discipline. Remember, while energy and patience are vital in reaching our goals, determination adds that necessary backbone and provides a firm grounding that nurtures discipline and sustained effort over time. Allow it to be your anchor, a point of return when you find yourself drifting, helping you to recenter and move forward with renewed vigor and purpose.

Ninth Paramis: Loving-kindness (Mettā)

This Paramis encourages us to foster a heart full of compassion and benevolence, not just toward our loved ones but to all life forms, wishing them happiness and well-being.

In a time when society is often polarized and divisive, embodying loving-kindness can be a beacon of light to guide us through the darkness. It invites us to extend our goodwill even to those we consider foes, encouraging a culture of understanding and unity.

To be clear, this does not entail fostering "toxic positivity" or negating bad feelings—rather, it's a gentle reminder to ourselves that we should not let hatred consume us. The practice underscores the transient nature of emotions, urging us not to harbor ill feelings and emphasizing the positive impacts of doing good, not just for others but for our own peace of mind as well.

Begin your day with a loving-kindness meditation where you take a few quiet moments to wish well for others—be it your family, friends, or even strangers and foes. Picture yourself sending them positive energy, happiness, and peace, fostering a spirit of universal goodwill, and nurturing a heart that is not burdened by hatred.

It is a conscious practice to remember that doing good, even when it feels undeserved, eventually cultivates goodness within you and radiates it out into the world. It is a daily practice of remembering that everything passes and maintaining a kind heart can be your anchor in turbulent times.

Tenth Paramis: Equanimity (Upekkhā)

This quality encourages us to nurture a balanced and steady mind, one that remains undisturbed by the whirlpool of external events or the storm of internal emotions, and to maintain a poised and serene demeanor in the face of life's oscillations.

Drawing parallels with stoicism, equanimity prompts us to avoid being carried away by the extremes of joy and sorrow, success and failure. Equanimity, like loving-kindness, advises a balanced approach where you acknowledge all feelings without letting them dictate your inner peace. It empowers you to manage life's uncertainties with a composed heart and mind, and mitigate undue stress and anxiety that can stem from a reactive approach to fluctuating circumstances.

To foster this balanced perspective, engage in a meditative practice where you envision yourself as a steady rock amidst a turbulent storm, unaffected by the chaos surrounding you. Picture the events and emotions as passing clouds, observing them without attachment, as you remain grounded and firm in your serene core.

This visualization helps you cultivate a state of stability, encouraging a centered approach to life where your inner peace is not easily disrupted by external factors. It's a gentle nudge toward developing a resilient spirit that can weather life's ups and downs with grace and foresight, nurturing a calm space within you, from where you can operate with wisdom and understanding.

Embarking on the path of cultivating the Ten Paramis sets us on a journey of personal growth and enlightenment, aligning us with virtues that have stood the test of time and transcend diverse cultures and traditions.

Each Paramis invites us to develop a quality that not only enriches our lives but also elevates our society; fostering a world grounded in kindness, understanding, and harmony. Through consistent practice and reflection, the Paramis guide us to become the best versions of ourselves; ready to face the modern world with ancient wisdom.

Reconciliation of Buddhism and Other Ethical Systems

The tapestry of the world's religious traditions is rich and diverse, with each offering a distinct perspective on moral and ethical living. Drawing from the heart of Buddhist ethical teachings, we find principles such as compassion, loving-kindness, and a committed approach to ethical behavior through adherence to the five moral precepts and the cultivation of the Paramitas.

These principles find echoes in the foundations of other religious doctrines, indicating a universal penchant for fostering goodness and nurturing a compassionate society. In this section, we delve deep into the common ground shared by Buddhism and other notable religious traditions, fostering a space of mutual understanding and respect.

As we delve deeper, we encourage you to refer to the insights gathered in The Review of Religions (2014) and GCSE Religious

Studies (2017), each a reservoir of wisdom and reflections from esteemed religious leaders across different traditions. These resources offer an enriched perspective and substantiate the discussions we are engaging in here, bringing forth the voices and understandings that have guided communities through generations.

Through this lens, we invite readers from different backgrounds to find common ground, understanding, and perhaps a kindred spirit in the principles and teachings that have stood the test of time, fostering ethical living and understanding in a rapidly evolving world.

Hinduism

In this exploration, we delve into the parallels and interconnected pathways that Hinduism and Buddhism offer toward ethical living and self-realization. These paths are guided by principles sourced from Hindu scriptures, specifically the Bhagavad Gita—a revered text imparted by Lord Krishna to the troubled warrior, Arjuna.

Drawing on the wisdom relayed by Mr. Umesh Chander Sharma, Chairman of the Hindu Council UK, it's imperative to underscore the universal nature of the teachings found in the Bhagavad Gita. Mr. Sharma highlights the pertinent theme in today's complex world—the necessity for a return to faith, advocating for a comprehensive adherence to the teachings that foster unity, understanding, and respect that extends beyond the Hindu community to mankind at large.

Much like the universal approach of Buddhism, which encourages us to undertake a journey toward enlightenment rooted in compassion and mindfulness, the Bhagavad Gita does not confine its guidance to Hindus alone. Instead, it shares teachings that are essentially a road map for life, advising how to navigate the labyrinthine corridors of human existence, and answering fundamental questions surrounding the purpose of life, happiness, and death. At the center of this guide is Dharma, a moral and ethical duty that also rings true in Buddhist principles.

Buddhism and Hinduism indeed find common ground in many respects, giving weight to the principle of ahimsa or non-violence, a doctrine that encourages adherents to abstain from causing harm to others, a clear reflection of Buddhist precepts that promote kindness and empathy.

In navigating through life's struggles, both traditions emphasize the role of personal actions grounded in humility, respect, and compassion. The Bhagavad Gita portrays this through its doctrines of Karma Yoga, the path of selfless action, and Bhakti Yoga, a journey of devotion—elements that find a reflection in Buddhist principles, guiding individuals in the direction of right action and loving-kindness.

Judaism

Judaism, rooted in a deep historical lineage like Buddhism, offers common ground in the pursuit of a compassionate, ethical, and sustainable way of life. Both traditions emphasize a deep respect for all of life and encourage an awareness of the interconnectedness of all beings. Let us delve deeper into this alignment using insights derived from notable scholars Rabbi Professor Daniel Sperber and Rabbi Jackie Tabik, representing the Jewish perspective.

Rabbi Professor Daniel Sperber delineates the Jewish orientation toward the world not as masters but as custodians, tasked with caring for it and preserving it for future generations. This reflects a spirit akin to Buddhism's emphasis on harmony with nature, selflessness, and loving-kindness.

Moreover, the Rabbi highlighted the concept of Sabbath—a day of rest—and the Sabbatical year, with its economic equality ethos, illustrating a mindfulness toward societal balance and justice which resembles the Buddhist emphasis on right livelihood and conscious living.

The Jewish emphasis on charity, freedom, dignity, and care for the less fortunate—termed as divine directives—echoes in the Buddhist teachings on compassion, ethics, and the alleviation of suffering. Rabbi Sperber points to a mandate of love, one toward God and another toward one's neighbor, urging a universal harmony grounded in mutual respect and recognition of the divinity in every individual. This notion parallels the Buddhist view of interconnectedness, where all beings hold intrinsic value and are intimately interrelated.

In the words of Rabbi Jackie Tabik, the deep-seated belief in the "oneness" that underscores the rich diversity of world faiths reflects the Buddhist understanding of interdependence, highlighting the need for fellowship, understanding, and celebrating the diversity while recognizing the inherent unity in all of creation.

Christianity and Catholicism

In the shared narratives of Christianity and Catholic Christianity, there lies a profound emphasis on love, compassion, and justice, a notion that is deeply rooted in the teachings of Jesus Christ. This spiritual path, defined by altruistic pursuits, harmoniously mirrors Buddhist concepts of compassion and loving-kindness.

Drawing upon the words of Archbishop Kevin McDonald, an eminent figure with a rich history of nurturing interfaith relations, we find an enriching perspective on Christian teachings that underscores the critical role of love and unity in the modern world.

By revisiting the Christian virtue of altruism, parallel to Buddhist doctrines of compassion and love, we find an opportunity to foster communities grounded in love and understanding. Both traditions significantly emphasize community service, with Buddhism endorsing a lifestyle steeped in generosity and moral living, while Christianity seeks to foster unity through charitable missions guided by the Church.

Archbishop McDonald reflects on pivotal moments of interfaith gatherings initiated by Pope John Paul II and Pope Francis, highlighting the transcendent purpose that binds all—peace and justice. Through collaborative efforts with religious leaders from different backgrounds, the journey toward understanding and mutual respect is continuously forged, aiming to build a world guided by shared values and dedicated efforts toward peace.

As Archbishop McDonald explains, the personal reception of peace stems from prayerful fidelity to religious truths. This creates a synergistic pathway for both Buddhists and Christians to foster compassion and kindness, leveraging the principles of mindfulness and moral living to navigate the terrains of suffering and uncertainty that characterize the modern world.

Islam

Buddhist principles and Islamic teachings share a profound alignment, especially in encouraging mindful living and championing the well-being of communities through generous actions and moral conduct. This synthesis of values reflects an interconnected universe where compassion, generosity, and mindfulness are central tenets in fostering a harmonious society.

In the insightful words imparted by Khalifa Hazrat Khalifatul Masih V, we find echoes of core Buddhist and Islamic ideals uniting. It emphasized that the pressing challenges facing humanity today, marked by uncertainty and inequality, can be mitigated through concerted humanitarian efforts guided by the principles of selfless service, compassion, and a deep sense of responsibility toward the community and its individuals.

Moreover, the Khalifa stressed the importance of serving mankind in two significant ways—bringing people closer to their Creator and aiding individuals in times of trials and tribulations. This dual approach mirrors the Buddhist practice of mindfulness, which encourages individuals to live consciously and deliberately, as well as a deep commitment to ethical living. This commitment entails bringing ease and comfort to those deprived and suffering, aligning seamlessly with the Islamic principle of Zakat, which promotes generosity and moral conduct through charitable actions.

Guided by a spirit of altruism and respect for all, irrespective of religious or ethnic backgrounds, the principles emphasized during this conference mirror the universal Buddhist teachings of compassion, ethical conduct, and understanding, forming a rich tapestry of wisdom that is both ancient and continually relevant in addressing the modern world's complexities.

Actionable Insights for Interfaith Understanding

To foster a deeper interfaith understanding, it is beneficial to:

- **Educate Yourself:** You can foster a space of mutual respect and understanding by educating oneself and others on the universal principles shared across various religions. Critically evaluate and distance oneself from extremist groups and views that distort the rich and harmonious teachings found at the heart of many religious traditions.

- **Engage in Dialogues and Interfaith Study Groups**: Foster spaces of learning and mutual understanding through discussions that explore the synergies between different religious teachings, whether informally or in a structured study group setting.

- **Collaborate in Community Services**: To make a positive impact, join forces with others in community services, drawing upon the common values of altruism and generosity. By working together, you can amplify the reach and effectiveness of your efforts, benefiting not only your local community but also fostering a sense of unity and compassion among its members.

- **Take Time to Reflect**: Dedicate time daily to personally reflect on ethical teaching from any religious tradition, contemplating its application in your daily life to foster a kind and compassionate self.

Through this journey across different religious landscapes, we find the beautiful interlacing of universal principles, encouraging us to live lives rooted in compassion, ethics, and mutual respect. Drawing from the rich resources of wisdom from Buddhism and other religious teachings, we are equipped with actionable tools for nurturing a harmonious society grounded in universal ethical principles.

As we wrap up this expansive yet insightful chapter, it is important to underscore that engaging with the ethical teachings distilled in Buddhist principles and those found in other religious traditions does not mandate a religious alignment or belief. Whether one identifies with a religious group, is spiritually inclined, or chooses to steer clear of religious affiliations altogether, there exists a rich landscape of ethical guidance that stands tall, unaffected by the passage of time.

These universal principles beckon us with a timeless call to embrace the higher virtues of compassion, understanding, and respect that can beautifully bind humanity in a warm embrace, transcending boundaries and differences. As we embrace these foundational truths shared by many spiritual paths, we find that it is more than enough to guide us toward a fulfilling life of harmony, respecting each other's shared and unique pathways in the grand tapestry of existence.

Thus, as we part ways with this chapter, we take with us a rich repository of learnings, a testament to the interconnectedness of ethical living that remains a beacon of hope—a bridge to bring people together in a world yearning for kindness and mutual respect.

Chapter 4:

Buddhism and Relationships

Relationships shape our experiences, beliefs, and our understanding of the world. From early familial ties to adult romantic bonds, friendships, and even interactions with colleagues, every relationship has the potential to teach us something profound about ourselves. Buddhism, with its nuanced wisdom, offers insights that can guide us through the maze of interpersonal dynamics.

In this chapter, we delve into the beautiful intersection of Buddhism and relationships, uncovering how ancient teachings can foster stronger, more fulfilling connections in various facets of our lives. Whether it's finding new relationships or nurturing existing ones, this chapter offers a guide filled with practical tips and enriched with Buddhist principles to navigate the sometimes turbulent waters of relationships with grace and wisdom.

Buddhist Principles in Personal Relationships

- **Understanding Anatta (No-Self) in Relationships**: As we explored in the opening chapter, the heart of Buddhist teachings is the concept of anatta, which means "no-self." This might sound counterintuitive at first, and you may be wondering how the idea of "no-self" relates to personal relationships. The correlation lies in the fact that this doctrine suggests our identities are not fixed and are subject to change. Recognizing this fluidity allows us to approach relationships without ego or attachment, leading to deeper connections.

- **Mindful Communication and Reflective Dialogue**: Right speech, one of the pillars of the Buddhist Eightfold Path, emphasizes the importance of speaking truthfully, kindly, and beneficially. In relationships, mindful communication means actively listening, being receptive to feedback, speaking with intention and self-awareness, and avoiding hurtful words. It ensures our words reflect compassion toward ourselves and others.

- **Compassionate Action**: Karuna, or compassion, is about recognizing the suffering of others and wanting to alleviate it. Every relationship can benefit from the infusion of more compassion, from understanding a partner's challenges to empathizing with a colleague's work pressures. Compassion ensures relationships are nurturing, understanding, and forgiving.

- **Reflection through Relationships**: One can gain insight into oneself by reflecting on relationships with others. Whether it's a deep relationship or a mere encounter, reflecting on it can provide an understanding of one's emotional responses, biases, and areas of growth. Furthermore, there's potential in recognizing the karmic dance hidden within our relationships. The forces of karma can teach us about the consequences of our actions, both past and present. Our reactions to others and theirs to ours provide invaluable insights into habitual responses, eventually revealing the dance of karma.

- **Understanding Interdependence in Relationships**: The concept of "interdependence" suggests that we don't exist in isolation. Every action, word, or thought

86

reverberates, impacting others and the world around us. By acknowledging this interdependence, we recognize that relationships are not just about give and take; they're a mirror reflecting our deepest desires, fears, and inclinations (Gucciardi, n.d.). A practical application of this understanding would be in a romantic relationship. Recognizing interdependence means understanding that the well-being of one partner inherently affects the well-being of the other.

- **Navigating Codependency**: Most relationships in samsāra, the cycle of birth and death, tend to be codependent. The concept of codependency in Buddhism suggests a habitual pattern of relating driven by karmic conditioning (Gucciardi, n.d.). For a relationship to flourish, understanding this pattern and striving for balance is essential. Such awareness prevents us from becoming trapped in patterns that breed resentment, misunderstanding, or neglect.

Friendship Through a Buddhist Lens

The concept of Kalyāṇa-mittatā, often translated as "admirable friendship," holds a prized place in Buddhism (Barre Center for Buddhist Studies, 2013). According to Buddha, good friends are not just a luxury, but a vital part of the spiritual path.

Just as we are urged to build a strong foundation within ourselves, the concept of admirable friendship advises us to cultivate relationships that are grounded in virtue, understanding, and mutual growth. This kind of friendship goes beyond casual acquaintances—it is about surrounding yourself with people who bring out the best in you, individuals who embody the principles of kindness, wisdom, and ethical living.

In this dance of interdependence, where relationships become a mirror reflecting our state of life, the quality of friendship holds a significant place. Engaging in discussions with people who are "advanced in virtue" encourages us to nurture positive qualities like conviction, discernment, and generosity within ourselves. It is like forming a community where everyone is encouraging each other to grow and flourish, promoting a culture of empathy, understanding, and constructive feedback.

It also means being cautious in choosing our companions, avoiding those who might lead us to destructive paths, and being vigilant about nurturing friendships that are warm-hearted, wise, and sympathetic. It is essential to remember that a true friend stands by you in happiness and sorrow, offering good counsel and understanding. They are there, supporting you, just as you nurture and develop the good within yourself.

Embracing the "No-Self" in Conflict Resolution with Friends

In the realm of friendships and professional relationships, applying the profound principle of "no-self" can also be a guiding light. When disagreements or conflicts arise, understanding the fluid and changing nature of the "self" helps us not to take affronts personally. For instance, in a conflict with a friend, instead of taking an affront personally, understanding "no-self" helps you see the situation from a detached perspective. This is not to say emotions are disregarded, but they're not the sole driving force.

Mindful Communication and Reflective Dialogue

The practice of mindful communication, reflective dialogue, and taking compassionate action further nurtures these relationships. Imagine a scenario where your close friend seems distant and less communicative than usual. Instead of assuming the worst or letting irritation build, you choose a calm moment to initiate a gentle conversation. You express your observation without blaming them, perhaps saying something like, "I've noticed that you've been a bit quiet lately. I'm here for you if you'd like to talk or need support."

In this setting, mindful communication is manifested through your conscious choice of kind and nonconfrontational words. Moreover, you're creating a space of trust and understanding, where your friend feels seen and not judged, encouraging them to open up. As the conversation unfolds, you listen actively, giving them your undivided attention, without the urgency to offer unsolicited advice or share your own experiences.

This kind of reflective dialogue allows for a deeper understanding to blossom, fostering a richer connection that is both respectful and empathic. Through this interaction, the friendship not only weathers a silent storm but grows stronger, with enhanced trust and understanding, affirming the strength of a bond that respects individual spaces while offering a compassionate ear.

Celebrating Others' Joy through Interdependence

Moreover, building on the foundation of interdependence, we come to perceive the joy and success of others, including our friends, as a cause for celebration rather than envy or competition. This realization sprouts from the understanding that we are all interconnected, and each individual's happiness contributes to the collective joy and harmony of our community.

For instance, when a friend lands their dream job or finds a loving partner, we find genuine happiness in their success, as if it were our own. This pure joy stems from the understanding that their happiness reverberates in the interconnected web we all are a part of, enhancing our collective well-being and adding to a more joyful, loving environment. This beautiful practice of being happy for others not only fosters deeper connections but also uplifts our own spirit, steering clear of the negative energies that feelings of jealousy and envy can foster.

Understanding Codependency and Karma in Friendships

Understanding the dynamics of codependency and karma can also play a pivotal role in refining your relationships. While karma speaks to the cause-effect relationship of actions, understanding codependency helps to delineate healthy boundaries; encouraging independence alongside interdependence and promoting a harmonious balance in relationships.

It is vital to acknowledge that while friendships are enriching and vital, maintaining a distinct sense of self and upholding personal boundaries are essential in ensuring relationships are balanced and not one-sided. Doing so will foster a landscape where both parties can flourish while being true to themselves.

So, as you navigate your relationships, be they with friends or colleagues, remember to walk the path of Buddhist wisdom. Not as a rigid set of rules, but as a warm invitation to foster connections that are rooted in understanding, respect, and deep-seated compassion for one another, thereby enabling a garden of harmonious connections to flourish and nourish your life's journey.

Nurturing Familial Bonds through Buddhism

Family—a profound word that evokes a myriad of emotions. Within a family, we find our first lessons of love, understanding, and tolerance. Yet, as the ever-accelerating world demands more from us, we sometimes find ourselves drifting apart from those who once formed our anchor. We need to consciously foster and nurture the bonds within our family to maintain its strength and vitality.

Buddhist teachings, with their emphasis on compassion, understanding, and interconnectedness, offer us invaluable tools to strengthen our familial relationships. Central to this is the understanding of love and compassion, as expounded upon by His Holiness the Gyalwang Karmapa (Karmapa, 2016). He offers a nuanced insight into how love manifests differently, ranging from the possessive love we often find in the world to the freeing love taught in Buddhism. This distinction is pivotal when exploring familial relationships, where love often intertwines with responsibility, duty, and expectation.

For instance, parent-child relationships, possibly the most profound of familial ties, teem with potent emotions. While a parent's love is often unconditional and protective, it can sometimes veer into the realm of possessiveness, especially when expectations loom large. By understanding love as taught in Buddhism, which frees one from fixation and attachment, parents can guide their children without undue expectations and children can honor their parents without feeling smothered.

Relationships with siblings, on the other hand, often present a tapestry of shared memories, playful banter, rivalry, and deep-seated understanding. They are our first friends and, sometimes, our first competitors. Embracing the Buddhist view of love and compassion, based on the common ground shared by all sentient beings, helps siblings see beyond petty squabbles, fostering a bond that's rooted in mutual respect and understanding.

Transforming Difficult Marriage: The Tale of Chieko Yamashita

Human interactions weave the tapestry of our lives, at times rendering vibrant hues of joy and at other times casting shadows of adversity. The dynamics of these relationships, especially during challenges, underscore the intricate balance of our emotional, physical, and mental well-being.

However, when faced with tricky relationships, our modern instinct often nudges us toward the escape route—considering options like switching jobs or severing ties with those we perceive as toxic. Yet, if the teachings of Buddhism were to be distilled, they'd preach a journey inward rather than a flight outward.

Chieko Yamashita's life seemed to crumble when her husband's business failed. Driven to alcohol and gambling, he pushed their family to the brink of despair. Their world spiraled into a whirlwind of debt, criticism, and even physical abuse. But amidst this chaos, a beacon of Buddhism urged Chieko to seize control of her happiness, leading her to an epiphany: The true power resided within her.

Fueled with renewed determination, Chieko immersed herself in the teachings of the Soka Gakkai. Miraculously, as her inner resentment toward her husband transformed into gratitude, he too began to find solace in Buddhism. Their shared journey through his health trials only strengthened their bond, painting a testament to the transformative power of faith and resilience.

From the ashes of adversity, Chieko rose like a phoenix. She not only redefined her relationship with her husband but also embarked on a journey of financial and spiritual prosperity. What began with managing a piece of land culminated in her owning a sprawling bicycle parking business and even establishing a community center, celebrated as the Yamashita Glory Community Center.

Chieko's tale is not merely a chronicle of enduring a toxic relationship—it is a deep exploration into understanding the intricacies of a difficult situation and transforming it through insight and courage. It is a vivid demonstration of the transformative power of awareness, empathy, and developing a belief in others: Showcasing how tuning into the harmony of one's inner wisdom can positively influence the dynamics of our surroundings (Soka Gakkai International, 2021).

Reflecting on this, it's clear that love cannot exist in isolation. It thrives in our mutual connections with others. Within families, love takes on various hues—from the protective love of parents to the camaraderie between siblings, the deep bond and partnership in marriages, and the reverential love for elders. By anchoring these relationships in Buddhist principles, we can elevate these bonds and ensure that our families remain our sanctuary, even in the face of external chaos.

Romantic Relationships in Buddhism

We traversed through the realms of family, reflecting on the heartwarming tale of Chieko Yamashita's marriage. Yet, before we embark on the journey of marriage and family, we begin at the genesis of a romantic relationship. Love and partnership have long been celebrated in cultures worldwide.

Over 4,000 years ago, love echoed in the verses of "The Love Song of Shu-Sin" on a cuneiform tablet, and today, the sentiment is immortalized in countless songs, from the promises of forever love by Ella and Louis to the pain of parting ways expressed by Taylor Swift (World Tribune, 2022). But what does Buddhism have to say about this universal emotion?

Buddhism teaches that true happiness isn't gifted to us by another but is an inner sanctuary that we must construct. It echoes in the words of the swordsman Miyamoto Musashi, who, while gazing at Mount Fuji, advised his students to first build a strong, unyielding core within themselves (World Tribune, 2022). Our relationships become the mirror reflecting our state of life. If we seek certain qualities in our partner, we should first cultivate them within ourselves. Love is a dance of interdependence, where each partner supports the other's growth.

Finding and Nurturing Relationships

To unravel the Buddhist perspective on love and relationships, it's necessary to recognize and appreciate several foundational markers:

- **Shared Dreams**: Genuine love transcends individual dreams, merging into a shared vision that acts as a compass for the relationship. It reminds us of the mutual respect and shared fascination for science that guided Marie and Pierre Curie in their journey of discoveries, symbolizing the unison of minds and spirits (World Tribune, 2022). In Buddhism, this concept extends to the communal aspiration of kosen-rufu, a shared mission to enhance the life state of humanity through spiritual practices.

- **Boundless Love**: True love is limitless and isn't confined to just two individuals. Such love becomes a reflection of boundless compassion, driving us to serve and support others. It is the love that pushes us to grow in ways that embrace all of humanity.

- **Growing Together**: A relationship isn't merely about companionship but also mutual growth. It should inspire us, give us hope, and invigorate our lives. Thus, it's imperative to ask ourselves: Are we challenging our growth? Are we better because of the relationship?

- **Admirable Friendship**: As we learned, the principle of admirable friendship is integral in understanding relationships in Buddhism. This concept urges individuals to foster friendships that are noble and virtuous, encouraging intellectual discussions and ethical living. Admirable friendship is seen as a cornerstone for cultivating virtue and wisdom, helping to navigate through life's journey with a mindset attuned to growth and learning. It emphasizes seeking friends who are not only good companions but also those who encourage moral, spiritual, and intellectual development, holding a mirror to our better selves and inspiring us to reach greater heights.

How do we know if someone is right for us? Buddhist teachings guide us to take our time. Instead of rushing into a relationship or marriage, these teachings suggest refining ourselves first so that we can be with someone who resonates with our core. Romantic relationships give us a platform to introspect, bringing out our deepest desires and refining our character.

Buddhist psychology further illuminates our understanding, emphasizing love and non-attachment. True love necessitates the release of control, fostering genuine interdependence. This nonattachment is neither about detachment nor isolation but about finding serenity through relinquishing control, and enhancing the quality of our relationships (Dias, 2023).

Navigating Relationship Challenges

In the journey of love, we often encounter challenges that seem like insurmountable mountains. While love is the foundation, relationships are built on many other blocks, including understanding, trust, patience, and wisdom to discern when to hold on and when to let go.

Relationships are a rich tapestry of complexities, and recognizing when to move forward or stay is vital. It brings to mind the story of Chieko Yamashita, who exhibited tremendous wisdom and endurance in navigating her marital life during tumultuous times, thereby influencing her surroundings positively despite her husband's challenging situation. Her story teaches us that sometimes endurance, coupled with a discerning mind, can lead to more harmonious relationships and personal growth.

While love is a profound and integral component, it isn't the sole sustenance for a relationship. A refined sense of discernment to recognize when to persist and when to gracefully withdraw is crucial when striving for a healthy relationship, as this calls for a balance of various elements.

Buddhism places a significant emphasis on personal well-being, encouraging individuals to continually assess whether a relationship fosters growth or augments suffering. It is at these crossroads of uncertainty that we find a rich ground to employ Buddhist teachings and practices, fostering wisdom and clarity through avenues such as mindful chanting.

Before making the profound decision to move on, it's beneficial to pause and delve deeply into a process of reflection and understanding. Here we offer you a compass, rooted in wisdom, to navigate this intricate journey (Dias, 2023):

- **Practice Mindful Awareness**: Regularly check in with yourself, noting moments of anxiety or insecurity. Recognize your impulses so you can take a moment to breathe and reflect before reacting. This offers space for healthier responses to emerge.

- **Seek Internal Security**: In the midst of turmoil, there is a sanctuary within that can offer solace. Remind yourself of your inner strength and safety, channeling affirmations that emphasize self-support and freedom.

- **Grounding and Analysis**: Before making a decision, ground yourself with the stability of the present moment. Analyze the situation objectively, exploring the dynamics without being swayed by transient emotions. The practice of grounding fosters a stable mindset to evaluate the circumstances critically.

- **Engage in Compassionate Release**: If the path leads to parting ways, let it be done with utmost compassion, respect, and mindfulness. This will allow you to cherish the moments shared and let go with a heart that wishes well for both.

As we close this chapter, we find ourselves enriched with a deeper understanding of the components required for a healthy relationship and practical approaches to cultivating fulfilling connections rooted in Buddhist principles. The journey we undertook through the vistas of personal relationships, friendships, familial bonds, and romantic engagements taught us the true essence of understanding, compassion, and harmonious living.

Stepping into the next chapter, we venture into a fascinating exploration of Buddhism's perspective on a very pertinent topic in today's fast-paced world—modern technology. We will unearth how the ancient wisdom of Buddhism interacts with the digital age, guiding us to use technology not just as a tool, but as a medium to foster understanding, mindfulness, and a deeper connection with the world around us.

Chapter 5:

Buddhism and Technology

As we journeyed through the rich tapestry of Buddhist values and ethics in Chapter 3, we noticed remarkable similarities with many other traditional value systems. A distinguishing feature of Buddhism, however, is its profound emphasis on self-cultivation and accountability, providing a thoughtful and enriching perspective on how we can engage with technology—a tool that is double-edged and powerful, bringing convenience and challenges in equal measure.

With this great power also comes a great responsibility to use it ethically, safeguarding the rights and well-being of all sentient life forms. To understand the depth of this responsibility, we need to navigate through the rich well of Buddhist teachings. These teachings are grounded in compassion and the mission to alleviate suffering, providing a philosophical lens through which we can observe and influence the ethics and equilibrium of technology usage.

In this chapter, we venture into the intriguing intersection where ancient Buddhist philosophies meet modern technological advancements. From understanding the rich history of Buddhism fostering scientific endeavors to adopting the Middle Path approach to technology use, this chapter offers a tapestry of strategies to cultivate mindfulness and balance in the digital age. Let's transform our relationship with technology into one of growth, understanding, and deep connection.

A Journey through Time: Buddhism and Technological Evolution

In the early formations of our world, where communities were blossoming and ancient civilizations were forging paths of discovery, Buddhism stood as a profound philosophical guide, continuously advocating for progress and the nurturing of wisdom through varied avenues, including the realms of science and technology. It is through the interweaving paths of Buddhism and technological advancements that we see an enriching narrative emerge, one where spirituality and progress nurture a symbiotic relationship that has enriched societies over centuries (Tianzhu Buddhist Network, 2019).

Ancient Wisdom Meets Scientific Endeavors

In the ancient landscapes of Buddhist civilizations, there was a remarkable fusion of spiritual teachings and scientific explorations. Buddhist monks, scholars, and practitioners were often at the forefront of embracing scientific principles. They delved into areas such as medicine, where the understanding of the human body and its functioning was profoundly enhanced by Buddhist philosophies advocating for well-being and holistic health.

Pharmacology too became a focal point of exploration as Buddhist practitioners ventured into the heart of nature, investigating the medicinal properties of herbs and plants. These natural remedies were integrated into healing practices that have stood the test of time and continue to be relevant in today's world, serving as a bedrock for modern holistic and alternative medicines.

Moreover, the realm of astronomy was graced with the wisdom of Buddhist scholars, who sought to understand the universe in its grandeur by mapping the stars and contemplating the intricate patterns of celestial bodies. Their profound insights laid the groundwork for numerous subsequent astronomical discoveries.

Woodblock Printing: A Revolution Fostered by Buddhism

Taking a gentle step further in our exploration, we find ourselves immersed in the transformative era where Buddhism facilitated one of the most pivotal inventions in human history—the development of woodblock printing in East Asia. Buddhist monks and scholars were driven by a deep-seated desire to disseminate the enriching teachings of Buddha to a wider populace (Tianzhu Buddhist Network, 2019).

Motivated by the principle of widespread enlightenment, they championed this early form of printing, carving sacred texts meticulously onto blocks of wood, which were then used to print on cloth and later on paper. This endeavor not only facilitated the dissemination of Buddhist texts but also played a crucial role in the preservation of a vast body of knowledge, fostering intellectual growth and literacy in societies.

This invention was a testimony to Buddhism's nurturing embrace of technology that propelled dramatic transformations across spheres of society, nurturing intellectual awakening, catalyzing political revolutions, and facilitating deep-rooted religious understanding and tolerance. It gave impetus to a culture where knowledge became more accessible, steering societies toward enlightenment and informed existence, echoing the core Buddhist principles of wisdom and compassion.

A Guiding Light in Today's Tech-Driven World

As we stand in the vortex of the contemporary world where technology is often perceived through a lens of skepticism and harbors potential threats to our well-being, it is in the calming embrace of Buddhist teachings that we find a path of harmony and balanced integration.

Drawing upon the timeless Buddhist doctrines of self-cultivation and wise restraint, we find ourselves equipped with a philosophical compass to navigate the complex landscapes of today's tech-driven existence. Buddhism encourages us to foster a relationship with technology that is grounded in ethical engagement, urging us to utilize technological advancements with a spirit of responsibility, conscious choice, and humane understanding.

The Dangers of Overconsumption

The rapid influx of technology and the digital landscape pose unique challenges to our well-being and our pursuit of spiritual growth. As we navigate this environment, we encounter the Buddhist teaching that guides us to avoid the perils of overconsumption, a principle that finds immense relevance in today's world.

In a world of incessant notifications—a common reality for most of us, where our attention is constantly interrupted by the allure of messages, likes, and updates—the deep-rooted Buddhist concept of "attachment" meets us, offering a profound lens to view and understand the dynamics of our engagement with the digital world.

It whispers timeless wisdom that urges us to disentangle ourselves from the incessant pull, to free our minds from the clutter, and to cultivate a space of calm and centered awareness. Delving deeper, we are guided to reflect upon the phenomenon of digital addiction, a contemporary challenge with symptoms that reverberate through our daily lives, influencing our mood, self-worth, and even our relationships.

Buddhism offers a healing touch here, painting a clear picture of the consequences of this addiction through a spiritual lens, inviting us to be mindful of the paths we tread in the digital corridors, and encouraging us to foster healthy boundaries to protect our peace.

In this landscape, social media stands as a monumental entity, weaving a web of connections, narratives, and platforms where the "self" is constantly portrayed, refined, and exhibited. It is here that we meet the grand illusion of self, a space where the Buddhist principle of "no-self" can feel like a distant echo, serving as a gentle reminder amidst the whirlwind of selfies and personal broadcasts.

Yet, it is precisely in this whirlwind that the teaching calls out to us, asking us to uphold the challenging yet liberating principle of "no-self" in a selfie world. It urges us to delve deeper, to look beyond the surface, and to engage with social media mindfully. Additionally, it prompts us to recognize the transient nature of digital personas and encourages us to foster a true sense of self that is grounded, authentic, and connected to the deeper realities of existence.

As we embrace these teachings, we find that Buddhism offers not just an understanding but actionable pathways to navigate the realm of overconsumption. It is a gentle yet firm hand that guides us to moderation, helping us to discern the illusions from reality, avoid the trap of digital excesses, and walk the path of mindfulness by creating spaces of silence, reflection, and genuine connection amidst the digital noise.

The Paradox of Seeking Mindfulness in a Tech-Driven World

In the warm embrace of Buddhist teachings, we find an oasis of tranquility, a sanctuary from the ceaseless buzz and whirl of the tech-driven modern world. As we tread deeper into this exploration, we come face-to-face with a paradox, a dichotomy woven from threads of ancient wisdom and contemporary existence.

On one end of the spectrum, we have the demanding pace of the digital age, relentlessly urging us forward, fostering a culture of instant gratification with ever-present tech devices at our fingertips. Yet, even as we immerse ourselves in this rush, a part of us yearns for something deeper; something more fulfilling.

Here, the timeless teachings of Buddhism offer a gentle hand, guiding us toward a path adorned with deliberate slowness, beckoning us to embrace mindfulness in its purest form. It encourages us to unplug, sit in silence, and rediscover the joy in simple, undistracted moments of presence, cultivating a garden of long-term fulfillment that blossoms from spiritual practices.

This path, however, is not devoid of challenges. Our attention spans have fallen prey to the onslaught of technological advancements, constantly eroded by a barrage of notifications, messages, and updates. It threatens the very core of mindful living, pulling us into a vortex of distraction and away from the nurturing embrace of present-moment awareness.

However, let us also pause to appreciate the other side of this intricate tapestry. Technology, with all its might, has become a powerful enabler, a tool through which knowledge can be shared, and global connections fostered.

In the digital realm, a world of mindfulness apps and online spaces for spiritual growth bloom, offering avenues for many to begin their journey toward self-understanding and peace. It is a space where Buddhist teachings find a new home, reaching hearts across continents, breaking down barriers, and uniting us in the pursuit of wisdom and compassion.

As we stand at this crossroads, we are invited to forge a harmonious relationship with technology and learn to wield it with awareness and intention. It is about fostering a delicate balance between historic foundations and the use of contemporary technology, where we use the tools of the modern age to enhance our understanding and practice ancient principles to nurture a sense of connection and global community while remaining rooted in the rich soil of mindfulness and ethical living. Let this be a journey of rediscovery, where we learn to harmonize the rapid currents of technological advancement with the steady, nurturing flow of spiritual practices.

As we delve deeper, we find that at the heart of this paradox lies a beautiful potential, a symbiotic relationship where technology and mindfulness coexist, complementing and enriching each other in a dance of harmony, guiding us toward a life of depth, understanding, and fulfilled potential.

Balancing Technology Use with Buddhist Principles

In the ever-buzzing digital age, aligning ourselves with the rich teachings of Buddhism invites us into a sanctuary of equilibrium and groundedness. This can be seen as a form of self-cultivation, a practice of self-awareness and intentionality in the midst of contemporary challenges.

The Middle Path Approach to Technology

As we navigate our screen-filled world, the concept of the Middle Path can serve as our guiding principle. It encourages us not to relinquish technology entirely but to use it judiciously, finding that golden mean where technology serves us, and not the other way round.

Our smartphones, tablets, and laptops can thus transform from mere gadgets into tools that foster growth, learning, and connection. It is through this lens that we embrace technology, always aiming to use it for constructive, mindful engagement while steering clear of mindless consumption.

The 10-Minute Mindful Tech Challenge

- **Objective**: Foster self-awareness and intentionality during screen time.

- **Practice**: Before diving into any digital task, take a moment to set an intention. Ask yourself: "Why am I using this device?" After your task, take 10 minutes to reflect on your experience. Did you find yourself mindlessly scrolling or were you aligned with your initial purpose?

- **Tip**: Setting a timer or using apps like "Forest" can be a helpful way to ensure you remain focused during your designated tech time.

Mindful Consumption of Content

Dwelling deeper, we start to appreciate the essence of mindful consumption of content. Buddhism implores us to foster the Right View and Right Intention in every aspect of life, and our digital interactions are no exception. This involves making careful choices about the content we expose ourselves to and aligning our digital explorations with our inner values and aspirations for growth.

Curated Digital Consumption List

- **Objective**: Ensure that content aligns with your personal growth and values.

- **Practice**: Once a week, review the content you've consumed. Unfollow, unsubscribe, or remove any sources that do not align with your values or contribute positively to your life. Create lists or folders for content that uplifts, educates, and inspires you.

Setting Boundaries: Digital Detoxes and Mindful Tech Breaks

The road to self-cultivation travels through the land of self-regulation. Here, we learn to adopt digital detoxes and mindful tech breaks by integrating regular intervals to disconnect and recenter. Such mindful pauses from the digital humdrum allow us to nourish our inner selves, granting us the space to breathe, reflect, and simply be.

With heightened awareness, we learn to set intentional boundaries with our devices, reclaiming control over our time and energy. It is a gentle reminder to ourselves that while technology is a useful servant, it should never become a consuming master.

Digital Sabbaticals

- **Objective**: Regularly detox from technology to rejuvenate.

- **Practice**: Dedicate one day a week (or even just a few hours) as a digital furlough. During this time, engage in activities that nourish your soul—be it reading, nature walks, meditation, or spending time with loved ones.

- **Tip**: Inform close friends and family about your tech-free intervals so they respect and support your boundary-setting.

Harnessing Technology for Spiritual Growth

Lastly, we come full circle as we explore the cornucopia of tech tools that have blossomed to aid us in our spiritual journeys. Today, a plethora of apps and platforms foster meditation and chanting and even offer a deep dive into Buddhist teachings.

Moreover, we have mindfulness bells and reminders at our disposal, tiny beacons that help us integrate moments of presence amidst the digital chaos. These tools, when used wisely, can be allies in fostering a deeper connection with ourselves and the philosophies that guide us.

Digital Dharma Dive

- **Objective**: Harness technology to deepen your understanding of Buddhist teachings.

- **Practice**: Dedicate specific times in the week to listen to Buddhist podcasts, watch Dharma talks, or engage with meditation apps. Some recommended apps include

"Dharma Seed" for talks and "Headspace" for guided meditations.

- **Tip**: Remember to be discerning and choose content that resonates with your spiritual journey so you can avoid potential digital overwhelm.

By integrating these exercises into your routine, you not only enhance your digital experience but also root it in mindfulness, intention, and purpose. Each click, swipe, or scroll can thus become a step toward growth, understanding, and balance.

As we embrace the digital era with a Buddhist lens, we find that technology, too, can walk hand in hand with spiritual growth, inviting us to a path of awareness, kindness, and mindful living. It's a soft murmur in our hearts, encouraging us to forge a path that balances the rich tapestry of ancient wisdom with the pulsating rhythm of the modern world.

As we transition into the next chapter, let's carry this sense of harmonious blending into the green realms of environmental consciousness, unraveling how the Buddhist principles can guide us in fostering a nourishing and respectful relationship with our planet, nurturing not just ourselves but the environment that sustains us.

Chapter 6:
Buddhism and Environmentalism

With the knowledge we've gathered about the core ethics and principles of Buddhism, we can now delve deeper to understand how these principles resonate with environmental consciousness, laying the foundations for a green Buddhist practice. The blend of ancient wisdom and modern challenges is crucial, as Buddhist principles can offer insightful perspectives on contemporary environmental issues.

In this chapter, we blend ancient Buddhist wisdom with modern environmental consciousness to foster a green Buddhist practice. We explore the historical roots of environmentalism in Buddhist teachings, and how prominent figures in the Buddhist community today are merging age-old principles with current needs.

We will also offer practical guidelines on cultivating a sustainable lifestyle through mindful choices and actions, from the products we consume to the energy we use. Finally, we invite you to reconnect with nature through mindfulness exercises; nurturing a deeper, compassionate relationship with the environment. Let's delve deeper into this enriching intersection of Buddhism and environmental stewardship.

A Brief History of Environmental Consciousness in Buddhist Texts

Buddhism has a rich history spanning over two millennia, during which its teachings have been interwoven with countless cultures and ecosystems. Central to this history are the myriad stories that place revered figures, including the historical Buddha himself, in specific natural locales. Many of these tales depict pivotal moments where beings who were once adversaries of the Dharma underwent profound transformations.

These beings, which ranged from serpent spirits to dragons, eventually became protectors of Buddhism in their regions. In these narratives, the once adversarial spirits now guarded and upheld the teachings of the Buddha, contributing to the symbiotic relationship between Buddhism and the environment (Edelglass, 2021). Through ritual practices such as pilgrimage and offerings, Buddhists forged deep connections with their surroundings, creating spaces for Buddhist practice immersed in nature's embrace.

In addition to these narrative influences, the Buddha himself recognized the direct impact of human actions on the environment. Always attentive to the balance between spiritual pursuits and the well-being of communities, the Buddha laid down guidelines to ensure his followers lived in harmony with nature (BBC, n.d.).

This was not just about protecting nature for its own sake—it revolved around ensuring that communities remained unaffected by the actions of Buddhists. He advocated for a way of life that minimized harm to other beings, whether human, animal, or even the spirits of the land.

Therefore, environmental consciousness was reflected through the harmonization of communities with their natural surroundings, deeply intertwined with respect and reverence for all life forms.

The Core of Buddhist Environmentalism

The principle of interdependence stands tall in Buddhism, teaching that harming a part of the whole essentially harms the entirety. This philosophy has guided Buddhists to live in harmony with the environment, fostering a mindful approach to coexist with every element of the Earth.

Central teachings like the Noble Eightfold Path and the Five Precepts guide individuals to act responsibly, underscoring the importance of "right mindfulness" and compassion toward all beings, including the environment. Further, the idea of "do no harm" leads to a mindful and responsible engagement with the environment, creating a path for sustainable living grounded in non-violence and respect for all life forms (BBC, n.d.).

Additionally, the Buddhist concept of karma teaches that our actions, whether positive or negative, have consequences. This extends to our relationship with the environment. Every act of harm toward nature, whether born out of ignorance or greed, results in collective suffering, reinforcing the need for conscious and compassionate action.

While it's true that environmental degradation as understood today didn't feature prominently in ancient Buddhist teachings (Tricycle, n.d.), the broader lessons from Buddhism are deeply relevant. The path of wisdom and compassion, interdependence, and karma together paint a picture of how a harmonious relationship with nature can be fostered.

The Buddhist Approach to Modern Environmental Challenges

In contemporary scenarios, several Buddhist leaders and scholars have turned to the profound reservoir of Buddhist teachings to build a framework for an environmental ethic that is grounded in mindfulness, compassion, and a deep understanding of the interconnectedness of all beings. This deep dive into Buddhist ontology, cosmology, and rituals has the noble aim of crafting responses to the critical environmental challenges that characterize the modern era (Edelglass, 2021).

This evolving paradigm has been termed "eco-Buddhism." It harmoniously resonates with foundational Buddhist concepts such as dependent origination and interdependence, concepts which posit that everything exists in a web of intricate relationships where each entity influences and is influenced by many others.

However, this approach does not come without its critiques. Some purists argue that eco-Buddhism may be distorting the classical Buddhist traditions by reshaping them to suit modern narratives, possibly drifting from the original teachings and perspectives (Edelglass, 2021).

Despite the debates, it is evident that many Buddhists today are raising their voices louder in the environmental dialogue, taking a firm stand by reverting to the core teachings of Buddhism.

Eminent figures such as Thich Nhat Hanh, a global spiritual leader known for his teachings on mindfulness and peace, Bhikkhu Bodhi, a monk who has translated numerous Buddhist scriptures into English, David Loy, a well-known writer and teacher in the Zen tradition, and Joanna Macy, an environmental activist with deep Buddhist insights, are at the forefront. These individuals are pioneering efforts to apply the wisdom contained in Buddhist principles to address current environmental dilemmas, working to find a middle ground between ancient enlightenment and modern exigencies (Tricycle, n.d).

While it is true that the Buddha did not address modern environmental challenges—how could he, in a time so different from our own—the fundamental ethos of Buddhism, founded on principles of compassion, interdependence, and mindfulness, offers a uniquely profound perspective through which to understand and navigate today's ecological crises.

It encourages individuals to foster a deep respect for all life forms and to live in harmony with nature, promoting the idea that everything in this world is interconnected and that caring for the environment equates to caring for ourselves.

As we forge a path into the future, it becomes increasingly apparent that the ancient wisdom embedded in Buddhism might hold the keys to crafting a sustainable, harmonious future.

The tomorrow we endeavor to reach is built on respect for nature, where mindfulness shapes our interactions with the environment and guides us toward a path of understanding, kindness, and mutual growth. It stands as a beacon of hope, potentially guiding us to craft solutions rooted in millennia of wisdom and a profound understanding of the intrinsic interconnectedness of all beings.

Practical Actions Rooted in Buddhist Principles

In a world where the consequences of our actions reverberate in unseen and unforeseen ways, it is vital to tread lightly and with conscious intent. Buddhism offers a rich tapestry of teachings that can guide us toward making eco-friendly choices rooted in time-honored principles. Here we delve into practical actions one can take to cultivate a sustainable lifestyle by anchoring our habits in Buddhist ethics:

Building a Sustainable Lifestyle

Mindful Consumption

Drawing upon the Buddhist concept of mindfulness, we encourage readers to cultivate awareness of their consumption habits. This could involve opting for products made with sustainable materials, reducing single-use plastics, and recycling wherever possible. Consider performing a simple ritual before making a purchase such as pausing to consider whether the item is necessary and reflecting on the journey it took to reach you. This mindful approach promotes a thoughtful and reduced waste lifestyle, helping to foster a deeper connection between individuals and the environment.

Responsible Energy Use

As stewards of our planet, we must make responsible choices regarding energy use. Buddhist teachings advocate for harmony with nature, a principle that extends to the way we consume energy. Simple, actionable steps such as switching to energy-efficient appliances, utilizing natural light during the day, and being diligent about turning off lights and electronic devices when not in use can make a significant difference. Moreover, one might consider transitioning to renewable energy sources, such as solar or wind power, to further lessen their environmental impact.

Embracing Minimalism

Buddhism espouses the virtue of simplicity and the joy that comes from leading a minimalist lifestyle. It encourages us to shed excess and focus on the essentials, finding satisfaction in the present moment rather than constantly seeking more. You can start by decluttering your living space, donating items you no longer use, and adopting a philosophy of "less is more." Through these practices, one cultivates a space that is both physically and mentally liberating, fostering inner peace and a deeper connection to one's surroundings.

Gardening and Planting with a Buddhist Approach

Creating a garden is an act of harmony, a beautiful expression of the Buddhist principle of interconnectedness. As you plant seeds, visualize the network of roots growing underground, connecting and communicating with other life forms. Choose native plants that support local ecosystems and create habitats for beneficial wildlife. Apply the principles of Zen gardening, considering the balance of elements and the flow of energy in your space. Incorporate elements of meditation into your gardening routine. Use this time to ground yourself and connect with the Earth, nurturing a relationship of mutual respect and reciprocity with the land.

Beyond personal practices, we can extend our compassion for nature through community initiatives. Engaging with your community to create green spaces can be a fulfilling endeavor. Consider organizing or participating in:

- **Neighborhood Garden Projects**: Collaborate with neighbors or community groups to transform vacant lots or underused spaces into thriving gardens. Whether it's a vegetable patch, a butterfly garden, or a serene meditation spot, these green oases become hubs of connection—both among community members and with nature.

- **Biodiversity Drives**: Organize or participate in drives to plant native species, create habitats for local wildlife, or clean up local water bodies. These collective actions not only benefit the environment but also foster a shared sense of purpose and kinship among participants.

Guided Mindfulness and Meditation Exercises to Reconnect with Nature

Stepping into the embrace of nature can be a therapeutic and enlightening experience. We can nurture our connection with nature through guided mindfulness exercises that encourage us to engage all our senses. Here are some exercises you might try:

- **Sensory Nature Walk**: Begin by finding a natural setting—a park, a forest, a garden, or even your backyard. As you walk, deliberately slow your pace and engage each of your senses one by one. Listen to the rustle of leaves, the chirping of birds, or the hum of insects. Feel the texture of the bark, the softness of the grass, or the coolness of a stream. Inhale the fragrances of flowers or the earthiness after rain. By immersing yourself fully, you're not only appreciating nature's gifts but also cultivating a sense of oneness with the environment.

- **Sunrise or Sunset Meditation**: Position yourself where you can observe the sun rising or setting. As the sky changes hues, breathe deeply and synchronize your breath with the ebb and flow of nature's rhythms. This practice helps to center oneself and appreciate the cyclic nature of life.

- **Tree Meditation**: Choose a tree and sit comfortably nearby or under it. Close your eyes and imagine yourself as the tree, envision your body with deep roots anchoring into the Earth and your limbs gracefully stretching toward the sky. Feel the tree's strength and stability, its silent communion with the world. By embodying the essence of the tree, you nurture a profound kinship with the natural world.

- **Loving-Kindness Practice**: In a quiet space, close your eyes and direct loving and kind thoughts toward yourself. Once you feel immersed in this feeling, extend these thoughts outward—first to loved ones, then acquaintances, and eventually to all living beings, including plants, animals, and even the elements. This practice expands one's circle of compassion, fostering a holistic appreciation for all forms of life.

By acting deliberately and drawing from the profound wisdom of Buddhism, we can all contribute to a future where harmony, respect, and sustainability are not just ideals, but a lived reality. It is a journey of both personal and collective transformation, a path of aligning our actions with the higher principles of compassion, interconnectedness, and mindfulness; carving out a sustainable and harmonious path for generations to come.

As we close this chapter on Buddhism and environmentalism, we find ourselves standing at the intersection of ancient wisdom and modern practices. The time-tested principles of Buddhism not only guide us in nurturing a deeper connection with our inner selves but also invite us to forge a harmonious relationship with the environment.

As we step into the next chapter, we extend this nurturing approach to exploring guidance on practicing Buddhism in the diverse and dynamic landscapes of the modern world, including finding solace and community in solitary practice.

Join us as we navigate the ways to cultivate a fulfilling Buddhist practice in contemporary settings, even in the absence of a Buddhist community, bridging the old and the new in a path of self-discovery and mindful living.

Chapter 7:
Practicing Buddhism Today

In a world bustling with demands and distractions, the nurturing haven of spiritual practice can often seem like a distant dream. Yet, here lies the secret to standing firm amidst the chaos—carving out an oasis of serenity within ourselves, grounded in the rich soils of Buddhist teachings.

As we embark on this chapter of practicing Buddhism in our modern lives, we find ourselves at the confluence of age-old traditions and contemporary settings, perhaps sometimes even in the absence of a Buddhist community. It is a personal journey where the inner self meets divine teachings, where solitude meets contemplation, and where communal bonds are either a supportive force or a wistful longing.

To hold onto spirituality amidst the relentless currents of daily commitments requires a strong anchor—a practice that not only resonates with the heart but is also nimble enough to weave seamlessly into the fabric of our routine lives. The beauty of Buddhism lies in its gentle yet profound approach to life—a path of moderation that doesn't ask for renunciation of worldly pleasures but rather guides us to engage with them mindfully and ethically.

The secret of maintaining a thriving spiritual practice in busy lives is, indeed, rooted in the teachings of Buddha. It involves embracing mindfulness that grounds us in the here and now, cultivating compassion that opens our hearts to the world, and fostering a community spirit that nurtures collective wisdom and harmonious living, whether in physical gatherings or virtual spaces.

As we forge ahead, you will find pearls of wisdom to hold close in various landscapes of modern life, whether it is finding or starting a Buddhist community, sustaining your practice in solitude, or harmonizing Buddhism with other religious beliefs you hold dear.

In this space, we invite you to gather tools and insights to cultivate a daily practice that feels authentic and resonant with your being, even amidst our busy modern lives. The focus here is on how to practically integrate Buddhist teachings into our day-to-day experiences, leveraging the ancient wisdom to cultivate a rich, mindful, and compassionate life today.

Let's take a step forward, bringing along a heart filled with eagerness and a spirit ready to embrace the gentle nudges and profound insights of Buddhism in today's ever-evolving world.

Building and Finding Buddhist Communities

Since we live in a world where individuality is often emphasized, we sometimes forget the innate human craving for community and shared experiences. Venturing into the path of spiritual growth doesn't always mean a journey undertaken in solitude. There exists a rich tapestry of experiences to be had when we walk this path hand in hand with others; sharing insights, joys, and even moments of doubt.

The Joy and Benefits of a Shared Spiritual Journey

Embarking on a spiritual journey often opens doors to profound self-awareness and connection with the universe. It's an intimate exploration of one's soul, the meaning of existence, and the interplay of life's energies. Yet, when this exploration is done in tandem with others, it carries with it an array of distinct joys and benefits.

Numerous factors influence how individuals perceive their lives, from personal characteristics that define our personalities to the values we hold dear. Significantly, the role of spirituality and religiosity in shaping our self-perceived well-being has garnered considerable attention. Research suggests that spirituality and religiosity have a positive impact on various psychosocial and health-related outcomes throughout our lives (Villani et al., 2019). Such spiritual experiences amplify these positive effects, especially when shared with a community. This fosters a synergy that elevates the collective consciousness.

A community provides a canvas where shared experiences come alive, weaving a rich narrative filled with shared joy and collective learning. This interaction, influenced partly by the reverence for the Buddhist texts and philosophies, finds an echo in the everyday verbal exchanges of its followers.

According to a large-scale sociolinguistic analysis, it was found that Buddhists, much like adherents of other religions, significantly utilized more positive words in contrast to negative ones in their daily engagements on social media platforms. This pattern seems to mirror the overall encouraging and uplifting language found in popular Buddhist texts, showcasing the gentle yet profound influence these philosophies exert in daily life (Chen & Huang, 2019).

As Buddhists, engaging in vibrant communities (both online and offline) can further foster this positive narrative, creating spaces brimming with positive verbal expressions and encouraging dialogues. These environments resonate with the tranquility and optimistic lens through which Buddhism teaches its followers to view the world, further enhancing the joy and benefits derived from being part of such communities.

Moreover, being a part of a community instills a sense of belonging, a refuge where individual narratives merge into a collective symphony, and personal joys multiply as they are shared with others. In a Buddhist community, you find a nurturing space that echoes teachings imbued with kindness, compassion, and mutual respect. These gatherings become a source of strength, embodying positive affirmations and shared happiness.

Creating a Space for Collective Growth and Learning

Buddhism, which is predominantly practiced in Asia, has a pervasive influence that spans the globe, firmly rooting itself in various cultures and societies. Most global Buddhists reside in Asian countries such as China, Thailand, and Japan. However, the practice has steadily permeated the West over the last century, becoming a vital spiritual path for many individuals far removed from its geographical origins.

But where does one find a community to foster spiritual growth in this widespread yet deeply individual journey? Thankfully, the world both offline and online offers rich possibilities.

In many cities and towns, traditional Buddhist monasteries, temples, and meditation centers welcome individuals with open arms, offering a treasure trove of learning and connections. Attending sessions, engaging in retreats, and immersing yourself in the nurturing environments of these centers can be deeply enriching experiences. If you have the opportunity, seek them out and become a part of their vibrant communities.

But what if there are no Buddhist centers in your vicinity or if physical attendance isn't possible due to other constraints? The modern age offers a solution through the digital realm. You can take the initiative to start a local meditation group, even if it initially involves a small circle of friends. Furthermore, the online sphere teems with platforms where you can connect with fellow enthusiasts worldwide, paving the way for virtual sanghas (Buddhist communities) that erase geographical boundaries and unite hearts globally.

As you cultivate this newfound community, bear in mind the principles of Buddhism to create a space resonating with harmony, openness, and mutual respect. A place where diverse interpretations of Buddhism are celebrated, where questions are not just welcomed but encouraged; fostering a fertile ground for shared growth and exploration. Delve into the teachings, the texts, and the practices together, allowing each member to contribute their perspectives, learn, and evolve.

Building and finding a Buddhist community transcends numerical strength; it is about nurturing a space where every heartbeat syncs with the divine quest for enlightenment. Where each voice harmonizes in a symphony of shared learning, and every soul finds solace in the collective embrace of the Dharma.

Remember, the joy and fulfillment derived from a shared spiritual journey, as evidenced by a growing body of research, enhance many aspects of individual well-being and foster a profound sense of contentment. It is indeed a rich pathway illuminated with collective wisdom and shared experiences, creating a rich tapestry of interconnected souls walking the path of Buddhism in the modern world.

The Solitary Practitioner

Walking the Buddhist path is as unique as every heartbeat, as individual as every breath. While being a part of a community has its undeniable advantages, which we've delved into earlier, taking a solitary route is not only equally valid but can offer its own set of profound insights and personal growth. If you've chosen, or circumstances have led you to embrace the role of a solitary practitioner, it's crucial to recognize the power and potential of this choice and, fear not, for the universe brims with resources to aid your journey.

Crafting a Personal Spiritual Routine

Taking the initial steps on the Buddhist path alone can be an enriching experience, fostering deep personal connections with the teachings. Start by setting aside a sacred time each day dedicated to your spiritual nourishment. This might involve reading a passage from a sacred text, engaging in a period of meditation, or simply sitting in quiet reflection.

Engaging with the rhythms of nature can also be a wonderful addition to your routine. Whether it is a walk amidst trees or pausing to appreciate the beauty of a sunrise, natural settings can facilitate a deep connection to the profound teachings of Buddhism. Also, remember to introduce practices that nurture compassion and kindness, toward yourself and others, integrating the core Buddhist principles into your daily life.

Online Platforms and Resources

In the digital age, a plethora of resources await to guide you on your solitary journey. From online courses offering teachings from revered monks and scholars to YouTube channels hosting guided meditations—the internet offers a virtual monastery at your fingertips.

Podcasts can be a rich source of teachings, allowing you to delve deep into various topics at your convenience. Engage with online forums or social media groups where fellow solitary practitioners and experienced Buddhists share insights and experiences, offering a virtual sangha to support and enrich your path. Libraries and bookstores, both physical and online, offer a wealth of literature to expand your understanding and nurture your practice.

Make sure to explore apps that cater to mindfulness enthusiasts, offering guided meditations, dharma talks, and tools to help you remain grounded in your practice. While engaging with these resources, remember to maintain a discerning mindset. Embrace teachings that resonate with your spirit and encourage respectful discourse.

As you stand on the threshold of deepening your personal and spiritual growth in the next chapter, remember that the solitary path is adorned with both challenges and beautiful solitary milestones. Crafting your journey with attentiveness and a spirit of exploration will not only facilitate personal growth but also pave the way for a fulfilling and transformative experience.

Interfaith Dialogue and Balancing Beliefs

As we unpacked in Chapter 3: Buddhism and Ethics, the Buddhist philosophy beautifully echoes many other religious and spiritual traditions, showcasing a common ground where understanding and respect bloom in a symphony of harmonious coexistence.

Respected leaders from religions such as Judaism, Christianity, Islam, Hinduism, and others have voiced the urgent call for humanity to come together in a warm embrace, transcending boundaries through the higher virtues of compassion, understanding, and respect.

Exploring the richness of interfaith dialogues opens a vibrant palette of understanding, where the foundational principles of Buddhism resonate harmoniously with the teachings of other traditions. Here, we discover a beautiful opportunity for growth, learning, and profound reflection. It's a place where questions are welcomed and dialogues are nurtured, offering avenues to appreciate the unity in diversity and to celebrate the shared ethos that binds us all.

In the pathway to personal and spiritual growth, many find themselves grappling with questions on how to balance Buddhism with other religious beliefs, or even the absence of religious affiliations. Thankfully, Buddhism offers a gentle approach to balance and harmony, encouraging us to carve out a path that respects and incorporates the richness of diverse philosophies, be they religious or secular.

Harmoniously integrating Buddhist teachings with other beliefs doesn't necessarily mean walking a tightrope of conflicts and compromises. It is about fostering an environment where the virtues of compassion, understanding, and ethical living seamlessly blend, nurturing a spirit of inclusivity and respect for all perspectives.

Whether you find yourself grounded in another spiritual tradition or navigating life with a secular mindset, there exists a harmonious pathway where Buddhist teachings can seamlessly align with your existing belief system, enriching your spiritual garden with blossoms of mutual understanding and shared values.

Begin with Common Ground

- **Empathy and Understanding**: Start your dialogue with the recognition that at the heart of most philosophies lies a deep reverence for virtues such as empathy and understanding.

- **Shared Values**: Identify shared values such as compassion, kindness, and the pursuit of wisdom, which are universally respected.

Listen Respectfully

- **Open-mindedness**: Approach the conversation with an open heart and mind, willing to learn and appreciate different perspectives.

- **Non-Judgmental**: Allow others the space to express their beliefs without immediate judgment or rebuttal.

Educate and Be Willing to Be Educated

- **Sharing Resources**: Share resources and literature that shed light on the core principles of Buddhism and encourage others to do the same with their respective philosophies.

- **Workshops and Seminars**: Attend or organize workshops and seminars that focus on interfaith dialogues, where various perspectives are explored and respected.

Practice Mindful Communication

- **Mindful Speech**: Use words that encourage harmony, understanding, and unity.
- **Active Listening**: Engage in active listening, where you fully concentrate on the speaker, understand, respond, and then remember what is being said.

Participate in Collaborative Projects

- **Community Services**: Collaborate on community service projects that align with the core principles of compassion and altruistic service advocated by Buddhism and many other philosophies.
- **Joint Celebrations**: Organize events where different faith groups can come together to celebrate shared values, fostering a sense of community and understanding.

Engage in Personal Reflection

- **Self-Inquiry**: Engage in self-inquiry to deeply understand your own beliefs and values, fostering a grounded sense of self.
- **Meditative Reflections**: Encourage meditative reflections that allow for a deeper exploration of shared human experiences and values.

Exhibit Patience and Perseverance

- **Time**: Understand that building bridges between diverse philosophies takes time and patience.

- **Continuous Effort**: Remain committed to the dialogue, understanding that it is a continuous journey of learning and growing together.

Remember that the goal of interfaith and secular dialogue with Buddhism is not to convert but to connect and foster understanding, respect, and harmony among diverse groups of people. Let's embrace the richness that diverse perspectives can bring to our collective spiritual journey, fostering a tapestry of shared wisdom and mutual respect.

In our exploration through this chapter, we delved deep into the beauty within both shared and individual journeys, illustrating that whether together or alone, there is a path carved out for every seeker. We also embraced the nurturing guidance that Buddhist teachings can offer in fostering rich, respectful, and harmonious dialogues across various faiths and secular perspectives, enriching our understanding and kindness toward ourselves and others.

However, as we close this chapter, we find ourselves standing at the threshold of a profound realization, a glimpse of the ultimate goal that Buddhists aspire to attain—enlightenment. It is a term that reverberates with deep wisdom and boundless compassion and has guided seekers for centuries toward a path of personal and spiritual growth.

As we step into the sacred grounds of our final chapter, we invite you to join us with an open heart and a curious mind. Within the final pages of this book, we will delve into the profound concept of enlightenment, unraveling its intricate layers and discovering how we can embark on this sublime journey in the context of our modern lives.

Chapter 8:

Enlightenment and Buddhist Goal

Throughout the previous chapters, we have delved deep into integrating Buddhist ethics and values into various aspects of our lives. We explored the transformative power of mindfulness, compassion, and ethical living in fostering harmonious relationships, contributing positively to the world and environment, mindfully using technology, and building a compassionate community.

Now, as we culminate our journey, we prepare to explore the quintessence of Buddhism—enlightenment. But what is it? And why, after millennia, does it still reverberate with the same intensity?

In this final chapter, we will unravel the essence of enlightenment, revisit the historical significance of the Buddha's journey, and reflect on its universal potential for every individual. We will navigate the modern search for enlightenment and delve into the preparatory steps of cultivating the mind and heart. Finally, we will discuss how to manifest these teachings in our daily lives, thereby bringing ancient Buddhist wisdom into today's context and realizing our inherent potential for enlightenment.

So, let's embark on this illuminating journey together, exploring the depth and breadth of enlightenment as we bring all our learnings into a harmonious dance of understanding, insight, and awakening.

The Essence of Enlightenment

Enlightenment, or "bodhi" in Pali and Sanskrit, can be viewed as an awakening—a transformative realization that pierces the veil of our everyday perceptions and beliefs. It is the profound understanding of reality, devoid of the illusions and projections that our minds often superimpose on the world around us. Enlightenment means discerning the interdependence of all existence, seeing the intricate web that connects every being and every event.

At its core, enlightenment is liberation from the cycle of birth, death, and rebirth known as samsara. It is freedom from the chains of suffering caused by our attachment to an illusory sense of self, desires, and aversions. It's when we escape the clutches of the three fires or poisons: Anger, greed, and delusion (Tricycle, n.d.).

But while enlightenment embodies ultimate freedom, it is also the culmination of compassion. An enlightened being has boundless love, viewing each creature with the tender care one might have for their only child. Such a being operates from an inexhaustible reservoir of energy, communicating seamlessly with all, understanding the universe in its entirety, and acting selflessly for the betterment of others.

Historical Significance: The Buddha's Journey

The story of Siddhartha Gautama, who later became the Buddha—the Awakened One—serves as a testament to the transformative power of enlightenment. Sitting under a ficus tree in Bodhgaya, after years of seeking and introspection, he experienced profound insights during three phases or "watches" of the night. These revelations, which encompassed understanding suffering, its origins, and the way out, laid the foundations for what would become core Buddhist teachings: The Four Noble Truths and the Eightfold Path (Tricycle, n.d.).

However, the Buddha was not a deity to be worshiped. In a renowned early Buddhist scripture, when asked if he was a god, the Buddha responded, "I am awake." His enlightenment was not about attaining divine status, but about awakening to reality, rising above worldly conditions, and breaking free from suffering. He was a beacon, guiding countless souls toward enlightenment with his teachings (Tricycle, n.d.). Today, the statues of Buddha we see are not idols for worship, but symbols of what's achievable and reminders of the teachings that can lead us there.

A Universal Potential

It's crucial to note that enlightenment is not reserved for a chosen few. Every being possesses the potential to become a Buddha. Whether it's the Theravada tradition, where enlightened beings other than the Buddha are known as arhats, or Mahayana Buddhism, which sees every being as inherently enlightened but yet to realize it, the essence remains the same: All have the innate potential to awaken (Tricycle, n.d.xx).

This journey to enlightenment demands more than just desire. It requires ethical self-discipline, concentration, wisdom, and emotional balance. By refining our behaviors, understanding the impacts of our actions, refraining from destructive tendencies, and cultivating virtues like love and compassion, we inch closer to that illustrious state.

Yet, the path to enlightenment is arduous. It challenges us to go beyond our boundaries, question our deepest beliefs, and confront our most entrenched habits. But setting forth on this journey, no matter how challenging it may be, instills our lives with profound meaning and purpose.

Enlightenment remains the unchanged pinnacle of Buddhist teachings because it embodies the very essence of liberation, compassion, and understanding. It's not merely about individual salvation but realizing the interconnectedness of all beings and working toward collective betterment. As the Buddha's life illustrates, with unwavering determination and the right practices, enlightenment is within reach for all.

The Modern Search for Enlightenment

Today's rapidly changing world can make the ancient pursuit of enlightenment feel somewhat out of place. Yet, at its core, the desire for enlightenment remains a timeless quest for inner peace, understanding, and transcendence in a world filled with chaos, suffering, and distraction.

The challenges of the modern age are plentiful. We grapple with information overload, constant connectivity through technology, and societal pressures that often prioritize material success over inner well-being. With daily stressors and the tug of countless distractions, it's easy for the modern individual to question: "Is enlightenment even possible in today's world?"

Furthermore, misconceptions abound. One common fallacy is the notion that enlightenment—or what many understand as "nirvana"—is a place or destination, a tangible goal that, once reached, offers permanent respite from all of life's troubles. Some might see it as an instant panacea for all woes or perhaps a blissful state of uninterrupted joy. However, enlightenment is a profound understanding of reality, the nature of the self, and interconnectedness. It's not merely a fleeting emotion or state of euphoria.

Another misconception is that one needs to abandon the modern world entirely to seek enlightenment. While retreats and periods of seclusion can be beneficial, it's essential to remember that Buddha himself sought enlightenment while deeply engaged with the challenges of his era. Today, one can integrate the practices and teachings of Buddhism within their everyday routines, finding moments of mindfulness amid the bustle.

Many also mistakenly believe that only those who dedicate their lives to monastic practices can attain enlightenment. However, every being possesses the potential for enlightenment. It's about consistent effort, understanding, and the cultivation of compassion, love, and wisdom.

Indeed, there's a societal push to "do" rather than "be." This bias toward constant action can eclipse the contemplative practices essential for enlightenment. Remembering the value of stillness amidst the hustle is a challenge, but it's also an opportunity to reorient toward a more balanced existence.

Yet, the modern context also offers unique advantages in our search. The vastness of information available today provides an unprecedented opportunity to learn from various Buddhist traditions, teachings, and practices worldwide. Digital platforms host communities where seekers can connect, share, and learn from each other, transcending geographical boundaries.

Moreover, the challenges of today, from global crises to personal struggles, can serve as profound teachers. They prompt us to question, reflect, and delve deeper into our understanding of self and the world around us. In grappling with these challenges head-on, we cultivate resilience, compassion, and insight—essential qualities on the path to enlightenment.

As seekers on the modern path, understanding these challenges and misconceptions allows us to tread with greater clarity and purpose. The essence of enlightenment remains unchanged, yet the journey unfolds differently for each individual, especially in our current age. In the end, the modern search for enlightenment is a call to reconnect with our true nature. While the path may be strewn with contemporary obstacles, the potential for awakening remains, offering a beacon of hope, clarity, and profound understanding in an ever-changing world.

Preparing the Mind and Heart

Imagine setting out on a journey without any preparation: No map, no supplies, and no understanding of the terrain. Such a journey would be rife with unnecessary obstacles and difficulties. Similarly, embarking on the path toward enlightenment requires us to create a conducive environment within ourselves.

Even though many of us operate on autopilot; lost in a maze of tasks, distractions, and desires, the quest for enlightenment beckons for intentional stillness and introspection. It's essential to create moments in our daily lives where we pause, reflect, and nurture our inner being.

First and foremost, nurturing a sense of curiosity is vital. This not only involves gathering intellectual knowledge but also cultivating a genuine desire to understand the deeper truths of life and existence.

Next, developing patience is paramount. Just as a tree doesn't sprout overnight, our journey toward understanding and enlightenment is gradual, often filled with moments of clarity and confusion.

Lastly, being compassionate to oneself is crucial. As we tread this path, there will be times of doubt, missteps, and lapses in our practice. Rather than being overly critical, treating oneself with the same kindness and understanding we'd offer a dear friend can make the journey more forgiving and enriching.

Letting Go: The Art of "No-Self" and Detachment

As we learned, one of the profound insights of Buddhism is the concept of "no-self." It challenges our deep-rooted belief in a permanent, unchanging self or ego. Embracing this concept can be both liberating and unsettling, as it compels us to reconsider our attachments and the very essence of who we believe we are.

Detachment in Buddhism doesn't imply indifference or lack of care. Instead, it suggests a deep understanding and acceptance of the transient nature of life. This acceptance allows us to experience life more fully, unburdened by the weight of unnecessary attachments holding us down and liberated from the chains of desire, aversion, and delusion.

Remember that the path to enlightenment is unique for everyone. As you walk this path, there will be moments of doubt and difficulty. Embrace them without judgment. Understand that every experience, pleasant or challenging, offers a lesson and an opportunity for growth.

Enlightenment in Daily Life

The quest for enlightenment, often mystified and placed on a high pedestal, is more accessible and intertwined with our daily existence than we might imagine. Embracing this journey doesn't require us to renounce our day-to-day lives or responsibilities. We don't need to retreat to a secluded monastery, nor do we have to abandon our worldly duties.

Instead, the challenge (and beauty) lies in integrating the pursuit of enlightenment within our daily activities. Every interaction, challenge, and mundane task becomes a potential lesson and an opportunity for mindful reflection.

In the age-old teachings of Buddhism, the "Middle Way" exemplifies a balance between indulgence and asceticism (self-discipline). Translating this to our modern times reminds us to strike a harmony between our spiritual aspirations and worldly responsibilities. It doesn't revolve around getting lost in material pursuits or abandoning them but rather finding a purposeful, mindful, and ethical way to engage with the world.

Remember, everything you've learned about Buddhist ethics, values, and their applications in various aspects of life—be it relationships, the world, the environment, technology use, or the community—constitutes the path to enlightenment. Each of these facets serves as a stepping stone, guiding us toward deeper awareness and understanding.

Nurturing the seeds of enlightenment in today's context might seem challenging given the pace and distractions of modern life. Yet, the core principles remain unchanged: Cultivating compassion, practicing mindfulness, and developing insight. Simple acts, like taking a few moments to breathe mindfully, reflecting on our actions at day's end, or practicing active listening in conversations, can be powerful tools in our enlightenment toolkit.

One personal way to measure your daily alignment with enlightenment is to keep a reflective journal. Each evening, jot down moments when you felt connected, when you practiced mindfulness, or times when you could have acted more in line with Buddhist teachings. This not only serves as a reminder of your journey but also helps you identify patterns and areas for growth.

Thankfully, we live in an age where resources for spiritual growth abound. A myriad of books offer wisdom from diverse Buddhist traditions. Online platforms and communities create spaces for seekers to connect, discuss, and learn. These modern resources provide invaluable guidance, helping us bridge ancient wisdom with today's context. They allow us to adapt age-old teachings to contemporary challenges without diluting their essence.

Essentially, enlightenment in daily life is about conscious living. It's about viewing every experience, whether joyous or challenging, as an opportunity for growth and understanding. As we navigate the intricacies of our modern world, we can find solace in the timeless wisdom of Buddhism, using it as a compass to guide, inspire, and enlighten our path.

As we conclude this enlightening journey, we reflect on the timeless wisdom of enlightenment, the Buddha's significant journey, and the potential within us all. We've learned to prepare our minds and hearts, embraced "no-self" and detachment, and sought ways to integrate these teachings into our daily lives.

The insights and wisdom shared are seeds for you to cultivate in every interaction, fostering compassion, mindfulness, and ethical living. Continue to embrace Buddhist principles in all facets of life, finding fulfillment and deepening your understanding. Thank you for exploring the depths of Buddhist wisdom with us. May your path toward enlightenment be illuminated with insight, compassion, and growth.

Conclusion

Embarking on this journey through the pages of enlightenment and the wisdom of Buddha, we find ourselves standing at the crossroads of ancient teachings and the ever-evolving modern world. Together, we've traversed through Buddha's royal upbringing, his transformative encounters, and the awakening under the Bodhi tree. Each step has unfolded the core tenets of Buddhism—The Four Noble Truths, The Eightfold Path, and the pursuit of Nibbāna.

Delving into the second chapter, we discovered how these ancient teachings come alive today. The tools and insights bestowed by Buddhism have illuminated the path to mental well-being, practical mindfulness, and meditation. They stand as beacons guiding us through the challenges of today, inspiring resilience and inner peace. Techniques like breath awareness, body scans, and mindful eating opened doors to a richer, more present life, grounding us in the moment and the heartbeat of existence.

We then explored the ethical foundations of Buddhism, aligning ourselves with the Five Precepts and the Ten Paramitas. These guidelines became the compass for our actions, thoughts, and interactions with the world, fostering harmonious coexistence with diverse ethical systems and inviting a tapestry of interfaith understanding.

Infused with the wisdom of the fourth chapter, we nurtured profound relationships, mastered the art of mindful communication, reveled in the joy of every moment, and gracefully navigated the intricate symphony of human connections, creating harmonious melodies of life. We also discovered how Buddhism fosters love, understanding, and mutual growth by enriching our bonds with friends, family, and partners.

As we ventured into the realm of technology, we observed the dance between ancient wisdom and modern advancements. Buddhism offered a balanced perspective, a middle path that enabled us to harness technology for spiritual growth while remaining mindful of its potential pitfalls.

Chapter 6 was a call to environmental consciousness, a reminder of our inherent connection with the Earth. Here, Buddhism inspired sustainable living, mindful consumption, and a harmonious relationship with nature, inviting us to tread lightly and live deeply.

In the penultimate chapter, we explored the vibrant tapestry of practicing Buddhism in a modern setting, finding community, cultivating personal routines, and engaging in enriching interfaith dialogues. The solitary practitioner and the collective seeker alike found avenues for spiritual exploration and growth.

Lastly, we delved into the essence of enlightenment, a journey of letting go and embracing detachment and compassion. It was a reminder that enlightenment is not a distant goal but a present-moment realization, an unfolding journey within each heartbeat.

As we close this chapter together, let's envision a future where the seeds of Buddha's wisdom continue to blossom in every heart, guiding us through uncertainty and change. Envision a world where the principles of mindfulness, compassion, and ethical living are not merely practiced, but rather woven into the very fabric of our existence, illuminating a path of profound harmony and enduring transformation.

In this ever-connected world, let us foster a community of seekers and practitioners, where we share our stories, our insights, and our journey on the path of Buddhism. By using the hashtag #BuddhaInModernLife, share how these teachings have touched your heart, how you've incorporated them into your life, and how they've helped you navigate the seas of uncertainty and change. Each shared experience is a step toward building a community grounded in compassion, wisdom, and mutual growth.

And if this book has been a companion on your journey, a guide through the terrains of ancient wisdom and modern life, consider leaving a review. Your thoughts and reflections will help this tapestry of Buddhist teachings reach more hearts, more seekers, and more souls yearning for a beacon of light.

The journey doesn't end here—it is a continuous unfolding, a perpetual awakening. Whether you identify as a Buddhist, a spiritual seeker, or simply a traveler on the path of life, may you find the courage to walk with mindfulness, the wisdom to live ethically, and the heart to love boundlessly. Keep exploring, keep learning, and keep growing. The path stretches infinitely, and with every stride, you draw nearer to enlightenment.

Embrace Your Journey

As you reach the end of *"Buddhism Today,"* I want to express my heartfelt gratitude for joining me on this enriching exploration of modern Buddhism. Your presence on this journey is deeply appreciated.

Remember your complimentary copy of *"The Modern Meditator's Guidebook"* awaits! Simply scan the QR code. May it serve as a steadfast companion, nurturing your practice and understanding of mindfulness in your everyday life.

If the wisdom within these pages has resonated with you, I invite you to share your experience through a review. Your thoughts have the power to inspire others on their own paths of self-discovery.

As you continue forward, may your steps be illuminated with clarity and peace. Thank you for being part of this meaningful odyssey.

With boundless gratitude,

Olivia Rivers

References

Anālayo, B. (2020, May). *Somatics of early Buddhist mindfulness and how to face anxiety.* Mindfulness, 11(6), 1520–1526. https://doi.org/10.1007/s12671-020-01382-x

Barre Center for Buddhist Studies. (2013, November 30). *Admirable friendship: kalyanamittata.* Access to Insight. https://www.accesstoinsight.org/ptf/dhamma/sacca/sacca4/samma-ditthi/kalyanamittata.html

BBC. (2009, November 24). *Religions - Buddhism: Meditation.* https://www.bbc.co.uk/religion/religions/buddhism/customs/meditation_1.shtml

BBC. (n.d.). *What does Buddhism teach about the environment?* BBC Bitesize. https://www.bbc.co.uk/bitesize/guides/zc9bh39/revision/3

Bergland, C. (2022, December 2). *Buddhist precepts reduce stress and buffer depression: Study.* Psychology Today. https://www.psychologytoday.com/us/blog/the-athletes-way/202212/buddhist-precepts-reduce-stress-and-buffer-depression-study

Buddho.org. (n.d.). *The Four Noble Truths: Essence of the Dhamma.* https://buddho.org/buddhism/

Buddho.org (n.d. -a). *The 5 Precepts: Buddhism and morality.* https://buddho.org/buddhism-and-morality-the-five-precepts/

Channuwong, S., Ruksat, S., & Ploychum, S. (2018) *An integration of Buddhist teachings in stress management.* Journal of Community Development Research (Humanities and Social Sciences), 11(4), 148-158. https://www.journal.nu.ac.th/JCDR/article/view/Vol-11-No-4-2018-148-158

Chen, C.-Y., & Huang, T.-R. (2019a, February 6). *Christians and Buddhists are comparably happy on Twitter: A large-scale linguistic analysis of religious differences in social, cognitive, and emotional tendencies.* Frontiers in Psychology, 10. https://doi.org/10.3389/fpsyg.2019.00113

Dias, M. Z. (2023, April 21). *Transforming attachment patterns: Exploring avoidant attachment behaviors in relationships.* The Happiness Clinic Mental Health Blog. https://happinessclinic.substack.com/p/exploring-the-avoidant-attachment

Fronsdal, G. (2006). *Nibbana.* Insight Meditation Center. https://www.insightmeditationcenter.org/books-articles/nibbana/

Edelglass, W. (2021, June). *Buddhism and the environment.* Research Gate. https://doi.org/10.1093/acrefore/9780199340378.013.721

GCSE Religious Studies A. (2017, November). *Component 1: The study of religions: Beliefs, teachings and practices.* AQA. https://www.aqa.org.uk/subjects/religious-studies/gcse/religious-studies-a-8062/subject-content/component-1-the-study-of-religions-beliefs,-teachings-and-practices

Gucciardi, I. (n.d.). *Article: Personal responsibility: A Buddhist perspective on relationship.* Sacred Stream.

https://www.sacredstream.org/personal-responsibility-a-buddhist-perspective-on-relationship-3/

Karmapa. (2016, June 23). *Love and compassion: Transforming our relationships for the better.* https://kagyuoffice.org/love-and-compassion-transforming-our-relationships-for-the-better/

Mahabir, N. (2019c, October 30). *Advice from a Buddhist monk on how to start a successful meditation practice.* CBC Life. https://www.cbc.ca/life/wellness/advice-from-a-buddhist-monk-on-how-to-start-a-successful-meditation-practice-1.5341736

Monteiro, L. M. (2015). *Dharma and distress: Buddhist teachings that support the psychological principles in a mindfulness program.* APA PsycNet, 181–215. https://doi.org/10.1007/978-3-319-18591-0_10

Pignatiello, G. A., Martin, R. J., & Hickman, R. L. (2018, March 23). *Decision fatigue: A conceptual analysis.* Journal of Health Psychology, 25(1), 123–135. https://doi.org/10.1177/1359105318763510

Soka Gakkai International. (2021, January 1). *Building harmonious relationships.* SGI-USA. https://www.sgi-usa.org/2021/01/01/building-harmonious-relationships/

Tianzhu Buddhist Network. (2019, September). *Buddhism & technology: Historical background and contemporary challenges.* Department of Asian Studies UBC. https://tianzhubuddhistnetwork.org/buddhism-and-technology-historical-background-and-contemporary-challenges/

The Buddhist Society. (n.d.). *Paramis, Paramitas.* https://www.thebuddhistsociety.org/page/paramis-paramitas

The Review of Religions. (2014, June 25). *Judaism - Hinduism - Buddhism - Druze - Christianity - Islam.* https://www.reviewofreligions.org/10890/judaism-hinduism-buddhism-druze-christianity-islam/

Tricycle. (n.d.). *Does Buddhism promote environmentalism?* Buddhism for Beginners. https://tricycle.org/beginners/buddhism/are-buddhists-environmental/

Tricycle. (n.d.). *What is enlightenment? Can anyone be enlightened?* Buddhism for Beginners. https://tricycle.org/beginners/buddhism/what-is-enlightenment/

Villani, D., Sorgente, A., Iannello, P., & Antonietti, A. (2019, July 9). *The role of spirituality and religiosity in subjective well-being of individuals with different religious status.* Frontiers in Psychology, 10. https://doi.org/10.3389/fpsyg.2019.01525

Wongpakaran, N., Pooriwarangkakul, P., Suwannachot, N., Mirnics, Z., Kövi, Z., & Wongpakaran, T. (2022, November 30). *Moderating role of observing the five precepts of Buddhism on neuroticism, perceived stress, and depressive symptoms.* PLOS ONE, 17(11). https://doi.org/10.1371/journal.pone.0277351

World Tribune. (2021, September 20). *A Buddhist view of love.* https://www.worldtribune.org/2021/a-buddhist-view-of-love/

Printed in Great Britain
by Amazon